THE NZ SERIES

NEW ZEALAND MIGRATION

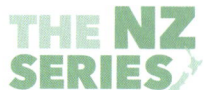

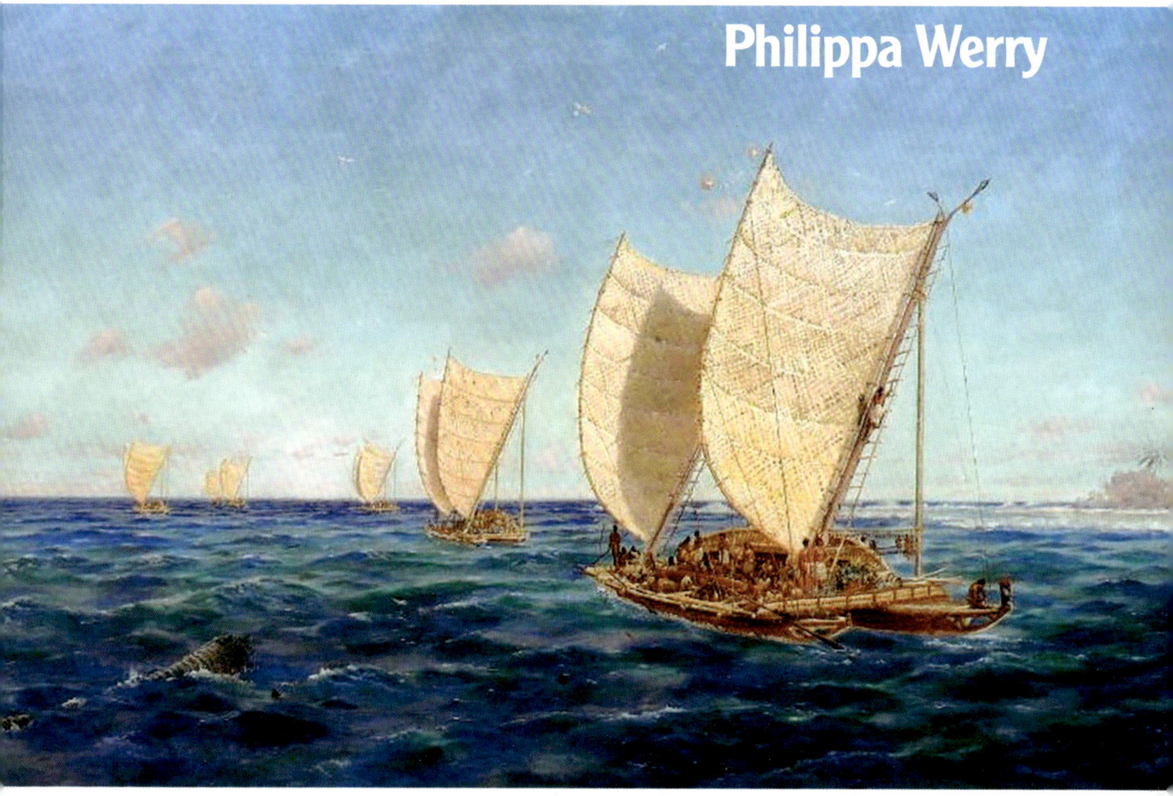

Philippa Werry

Oratia

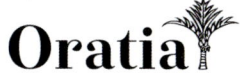

ACKNOWLEDGEMENTS Thanks and gratitude are extended to all of those who shared their knowledge, gave advice and provided feedback on all or sections of the text for this publication, including: Brad Haami, Lynette Shum, Nigel Murphy, Kirsten Wong, Manisha Morar (Vice President, New Zealand Indian Central Association), Nina Cuccurullo, Pauline Smith, Trish Harris, Basia Hanson (Secretary, The Polish Association in New Zealand), Adam Manterys, Gladis Ishak, Mariana Ishak, Ricky Prebble (Pouako/Educator at Pukeahu Education Centre), Dave O'Donovan (Stats NZ Tatauranga Aotearoa), Office for Disability Issues and Ryan Gray (Senior Communications Advisor, MBIE). Many thanks to all the wonderful librarians, archivists and historians who have fielded my enquiries, including those at the Alexander Turnbull Library, National Library, Archives New Zealand and Wellington City Libraries.
Finally, I acknowledge the bravery, courage and enterprise of my own migrant ancestors, as well as the sadness they must have felt in leaving family behind when they set off to New Zealand.

FRONT COVER Detail from 'Refugees arriving from Uganda, Wellington Airport, 1972' (full image on p. 83). Ref: EP/1972/5327/5-F, Alexander Turnbull Library, Wellington; Stuff Limited **BACK COVER** See pp. 12, 15, 56, 96, 90 respectively for image information **TITLE PAGE** Canoes leaving Rarotonga for New Zealand. Kennett Watkins, 1906 **PAGE 6–7**: The twin-hulled ocean-going waka, Hinemoana, Auckland Harbour. Michael Williams, Dreamstime **PAGE 62**: Young women, kaz_c, iStock.

All efforts to obtain copyright permission for imagery in this book have been made; any further information can be directed to Oratia Books. Some Māori words appear without macrons for historical correctness.

Published by Oratia Books, Oratia Media Ltd,
783 West Coast Road, Oratia, Auckland 0604, New Zealand (www.oratia.co.nz)

Copyright © 2023 Philippa Werry (text)
Copyright © 2023 Oratia Books (published work)

The copyright holders assert their moral rights in the work.

This book is copyright. Except for the purposes of fair reviewing, no part of this publication may be reproduced or transmitted in any form or by any means, whether electronic, digital or mechanical, including photocopying, recording, any digital or computerised format, or any information storage and retrieval system, including by any means via the Internet, without permission in writing from the publisher. Infringers of copyright render themselves liable to prosecution.

ISBN 978-1-99-004239-3

Managing Editor: Carolyn Lagahetau
Designer: Sarah Elworthy

First published 2023

The publisher acknowledges the generous support of
Creative New Zealand for this publication.

Printed in China

CONTENTS

Introduction 5

MĀORI DISCOVERY AND MIGRATION 8
The first arrivals 8
Adapting to a new land 11
Internal migrations and displacement 13

FIRST ENCOUNTERS, PRE-1840 14
Explorers, whalers and sealers 14
Traders and missionaries 17

'BRITAIN OF THE SOUTH' 19
1840s: The New Zealand Company 19
Soldiers and surveyors 23
1870s: Julius Vogel's Public Works and Immigration Scheme 24

CHANGING THE LANDSCAPE 27
Scandinavian foresters 27
Dalmatian gum diggers 29
Scottish shepherds 31

PREJUDICE AND DISCRIMINATION 34
Anti-Chinese legislation 36
The permit system 38
Other legislation 39
Aliens 40
The disabled 41
The White New Zealand League 42

MORE 19TH-CENTURY ARRIVALS 43
Chinese migrants 43
War times 46
Indian migrants 48
German migrants 51

IN THE SHADOW OF WAR 54
Jewish and war-time refugees 54
The Polish children 55
British child migrants 57
Chinese orphans 58
War brides 59
Cold War refugees 60

NEW OPPORTUNITIES 64
Ten Pound Poms 64
Austria 65
Italy 66
Greece 68
The Netherlands 70
Māori migration to the cities 71
Pasifika peoples 77

ESCAPING DANGER 80
Refugees and asylum seekers 80

1987 TO TODAY 88
Immigration Act 1987 88
Migrant workers 89
Colombo Plan and other students 90
The impact of Covid-19 on migration 92

CELEBRATING DIVERSITY 93

Conclusion 98
Index 100

*Like all migrants to New Zealand, whether they were
from Asia, Pacific or Europe, and whether they came on
canoes, sailing ships, ocean liners or aeroplanes,
they were all seeking to build a new and better life
here in New Zealand. As noted New Zealand historian,
the late Dr Michael King, wrote:
'In a country inhabited for a mere one thousand years,
everybody is an immigrant or a descendent of an immigrant.'*

Rt Hon. Sir Anand Satyanand
At the unveiling of the Edward Peters Memorial, 12 April 2009

INTRODUCTION

For millions of years, New Zealand was an uninhabited land of trees and birdsong. It was one of the last countries in the world to be discovered.

Forests covered the land like a green blanket. Bats fluttered, skinks and geckos scuttled, giant snails crawled and tuatara basked in the sun. Seals sprawled over the rocks, pods of whales swam up and down the coast and the sea swarmed with life.

Moa roamed the land. Giant Haast's eagles/pouākai soared through the sky. Kākāpō waddled along their tracks through scrub and tussock.

And then people started to arrive. Who were they, and where did they come from?

Giant Haast's eagle attacking New Zealand moa.

John Megahan

MĀORI DISCOVERY AND MIGRATION

THE FIRST ARRIVALS

Many Māori iwi tell stories of the great voyager Kupe and how he was the first person to sight this country while chasing the giant octopus Te Wheke-a-Muturangi. It was Hine Te Aparangi, his wife, whose cry 'He ao!' ('a cloud!') was the inspiration for the name Aotearoa.

The first explorers ventured here from East Polynesia sometime around 1200 to 1300. They were bold adventurers and expert navigators who sailed across Te Moana-nui-ā-Kiwa, the Pacific Ocean, out of sight of land for days on end, using the clues of winds, stars, weather patterns, ocean currents and migrating birds to steer their waka hourua. We don't know exactly why they made these long journeys. Perhaps it was due to warfare, conflict, growing populations and not enough food or other resources, or simply the desire to discover new lands.

Having crossed the seas, they continued their journeys of discovery over the land. Among them were intrepid explorers such as Tia and Ngātoro-i-rangi, from Te Arawa canoe, who travelled over the mountains, lakes and rivers of the central North Island. Rākaihautū, captain of the Uruao canoe, travelled south from Whakatū/Nelson to Te Ara-a-Kiwa/Foveaux Strait, traversing the mountains and using his kō (digging stick) to dig out lakes and rivers.

The first arrivals and their descendants gradually spread around the new country. They left no written records, but ways of working out when they arrived include oral histories or studying whakapapa. Radiocarbon dating can work out the age of found items made of wood, shell or bone. Scientists can test pollen grains preserved in the ground and calculate when man-made activities such as lighting fires might have started, based on changes in pollen in successive layers. Place names, myths of origin and even genetic testing contain more clues about the arrival of these first people.

Stories tell us that more than 40 waka made landfall within about a hundred years. After that, for reasons that are still unclear, long-distance sea journeys became less common. Some people

Kupe and his wife Hine Te Aparangi are immortalised in this statue on the Wellington waterfront.

Heather Cuthill

The brave Wairaka

Both men and women sailed on the ocean-going waka. Wairaka came on the Mataatua canoe with her father Toroa, the captain. The men went ashore, but then the waka started to drift out to sea. Women were not allowed to use the paddles but Wairaka realised they would be lost if she didn't act. She grabbed a paddle and took them back to safety, calling out 'Me whakatāne au i ahau!' ('Let me act like a man!'). The town of Whakatāne is named after her brave action, and her bronze statue, perched on a rock, is one of the few statues of women in New Zealand. Another woman, Whakaotirangi, is renowned in Tainui and Te Arawa tradition for protecting the precious kūmara seed on the long voyage, and for learning how to grow kūmara here in the colder climate.

The bronze statue of Wairaka, perched on a rock at the mouth of the Whakatāne River.

C. Lagahetau

moved to Rēkohu/Chatham Islands between 1300 and 1550 and their descendants, living separately from the outside world, developed the pacifist Moriori culture.

ADAPTING TO A NEW LAND

The new arrivals brought with them some plants, food and animals, such as the kurī (Polynesian dog) and kiore (Polynesian rat), as well as their culture and traditional knowledge, which they learned to adapt to the new terrain and new materials they found here. They had to acclimatise to an environment that was larger, colder and wetter than their former homes, with landscapes that varied from mountains, forests and swamps to geysers, mud pools and steaming lakes. They lived as hunter-gatherers, often setting up kāinga (villages) on the coast where they could harvest eels, fish and shellfish, forage for wild plants and roots and hunt seals, moa and other flightless birds, and then move on when the food ran out. They brought food plants from their Polynesian homes but some tropical plants, like taro, would never flourish.

Polynesian rat.

Buller, Walter, Transactions and Proceedings of the Royal Society of New Zealand 1868–1961, Vol. 3, 1870

This changed when food sources that once were plentiful began to vanish. By about 1450, moa had been hunted to extinction. The slow-growing population of seals had plummeted and kiore and kurī had made inroads on vulnerable flightless birds. People began to rely more on growing crops, especially kūmara. They cut down trees to make houses and canoes and built pā for defence if needed. They carved tools, weapons and ornaments from wood, stone, bone, shell and greenstone and wove flax into clothes, mats and baskets.

This new way of life, less nomadic and more reliant on agriculture, made it more important to identify land and its boundaries, which could be done by reciting whakapapa and the naming of places. Boundaries could be natural features such as hills and rivers or man-made

Putiki Pā, Whanganui.
Ref: C-142-003, Alexander Turnbull Library, Wellington

markers. Whānau (family groups) and hapū (subtribes) made up the network of iwi (tribes), often traced back to the waka on which their ancestors arrived.

INTERNAL MIGRATIONS AND DISPLACEMENT

Despite a more settled existence, with seasonal activities linked to the maramataka or Māori lunar calendar, trade journeys (such as on the greenstone trails of Te Waipounamu/South Island) and heke, or internal migrations, still continued. Competition for land, food and other resources led people to form new settlements. Migrating tribes fought with existing tribes but intermarriages also occurred. Older and more vulnerable iwi disappeared when they were attacked and killed or taken as slaves, or else they were amalgamated into new and stronger iwi and hapū. Some of these waves of migration in the 16th and 17th centuries took Ngāti Māmoe and later Ngāi Tahu from the East Coast of the North Island to spread over Te Waipounamu. In the early 1820s, Te Rauparaha led Ngāti Toa from Kāwhia to a new home after he saw the potential of Cook Strait as a base for trading with Europeans. This journey took place in stages: Te Heke Tahu-tahu-ahi (the Migration of Fire Lighting) from Kāwhia to Taranaki, and Te Heke Tātaramoa (the Bramble Bush Migration, named because it was so difficult) from Taranaki to Kāpiti. Many from Te Ātiawa also took part in Te Heke Mai Raro, or the Migration from the North, to escape attacks from other iwi.

For centuries, these people who came from a land they called Hawaiki were the only inhabitants of New Zealand. By the time the first Europeans arrived, their population had grown to about 100,000, and as iwi and hapū they had claims on or strong connections with land throughout the country. It was only with the arrival of the Europeans that they began to call themselves tangata māori, or 'ordinary people', to identify themselves as different from the Pākehā arrivals. Māori are the tangata whenua and the indigenous peoples of the land.

FIRST ENCOUNTERS, PRE-1840

EXPLORERS, WHALERS AND SEALERS

'First contacts' or 'first encounters' are terms given to the first meetings between Māori and Europeans. Many meetings were friendly, but there were also clashes and quarrels as the two cultures struggled to understand each other. Blood was spilt and people killed on both sides.

The first European explorers also arrived here by sailing into the unknown. Their maps showed a blank space at the bottom of the world, labelled 'terra australis incognita' or 'the unknown southern land'. In December 1642, the Dutchman Abel Janszoon Tasman sailed around both North and South Islands, calling them 'Staten Landt' because he thought they might be connected to land in South America with that name. Map makers renamed the country Nova Zeelandia (in Latin) or Nieuw Zeeland in Dutch. ('Zeeland' is a seaside Dutch province with several small islands.)

Next came Lieutenant (later Captain) James Cook in 1769–70. His ship, the *Endeavour*, carried not only sailors but also artists and naturalists such as Sydney Parkinson (who came from Scotland) and Daniel Solander (from Sweden). They painted landscapes, villages, houses and people, sketched birds, fish, flowers and plants and collected specimens to take back home. Cook had a Tahitian chief and priest on board, named Tupaia. The Tahitian and Māori languages were similar, so Cook was fortunate that Tupaia could act as a translator.

Soon afterwards, two French expeditions arrived, captained by

Jean François Marie de Surville and Marc Joseph Marion du Fresne. Cook returned later in the *Resolution* and *Adventure* (1773–74) and the *Resolution* and *Discovery* (1777). In May 1773, he wrote that Dusky Sound abounded with fish and shellfish, and seals could be found 'in great numbers.' Before long, sealers and whalers came to club the seals to death and harpoon the whales so they could sell the resulting products, including oil, baleen, ambergris and seal skins.

The first whaling ship arrived in 1791. The first sealing gang was left at Luncheon Cove on Anchor Island, Dusky Sound, in November 1792 with instructions to build a hut and a small boat in case their ship couldn't return to collect them. After that, parties of sealers were dropped at remote parts of the coast or offshore islands and left for months or years, enduring harsh weather

Group alongside a whale's head, at Te Awaiti beach, before 1895. Many of the people are descendants of the whaler Joseph Thoms and his wife Te Ua Tōrikiriki. In the background is the mail boat *Torea*.

Ref: 1/2-052158-F, Alexander Turnbull Library, Wellington

conditions with scant food apart from ships' biscuits, fish and seal meat. It was hard, dirty, dangerous work. Sealers and whalers had to be tough, and lucky, to survive, and many didn't. A whale could overturn a flimsy whaleboat with a flip of its mighty tail.

Some early settlers were seamen who jumped ship and stowaways, including Indian seamen and convicts from Australia who had escaped or served their time. A number of these men, called Pākehā Māori, became a part of local iwi. One of the first Pākehā Māori was James Caddell, the 16-year-old survivor from a boatload of six sealers attacked by local Māori on Rakiura/Stewart Island, who later married Tokitoki, the chief Honekai's niece. Some whalers married local Māori. Whenua Hou/Codfish Island in Foveaux Strait was the site of the first bicultural community in New Zealand. From the 1820s, it was home to local Māori women and their sealer, whaler or sailor partners and children. Traditional stories tell how local chiefs granted the use of the island to these families and gave it the name Whenua Hou, or New Land. Today Whenua Hou is also well known as a safe home for kākāpō. Further

Charlotte Badger.
Morghan Harper

The first European women settlers

Some of the first European women to arrive here were also convicts. Charlotte Badger and Catherine Hagerty, both transported to New South Wales, were on board the *Venus* when the crew staged a mutiny and sailed to the Bay of Islands in 1806. The two women were looked after by local Māori but Catherine Hagerty seems to have died soon afterwards. Charlotte Badger went back to Sydney a few months later.

north, John Nicoll, or 'Scotch Jock', married Kahe Te Rau-o-te-rangi, famous for swimming from Kāpiti Island to the mainland with a child tied to her back to warn of an approaching war party; she was one of 13 women to sign the Treaty of Waitangi/Te Tiriti o Waitangi.

TRADERS AND MISSIONARIES

Some Māori joined the whaling crews and others traded with them, exchanging fresh water, pork and potatoes for clothing, blankets, tools, guns and tobacco. Other traders arrived and opened stores to cater to new immigrants and ships' crews, especially in Kororāreka (today called Russell). There was also a busy trade in timber and flax, valuable natural resources that provided masts, spars and ropes for wooden sailing ships.

Samuel Marsden was an English chaplain and magistrate in New South Wales when he met the Māori rangatira Ruatara, Hongi Hika and Korokoro on their visits to Australia. He sailed with them to Rangihoua, Ruatara's home in the Bay of Islands, arriving on 22 December 1814. On Christmas Day, he preached a sermon on the beach based on words from the Bible: 'Behold, I bring you glad tidings of great joy.' With him were John King, William Hall and Thomas Kendall and their families. Their new home at Hohi/Oihi, near Rangihoua Pā, was the first Christian mission station and first permanent European settlement in New Zealand. By March 1815, at least 23 men, women and children were living there. The second mission station was in Kerikeri in 1819, followed by others in Paihia and Waimate.

Marsden belonged to the Church Missionary Society, or CMS, which was linked to the Church of England. It was founded in 1799 by men who worked to abolish the slave trade and promote peace. New Zealand was one of the first CMS destinations, after West Africa (1804), the West Indies (1813) and India (also in 1814). Other missionaries followed: Wesleyan-Methodist (from 1822) and Catholic (from 1838).

The missionaries learnt te reo Māori (the Māori language)

and played a role as peacemakers and translators. They travelled around the country and established new mission stations but made few converts until the 1830s. Their work was sometimes marred by scandal, discord and controversy, and some worked harder than others to understand the Māori world view. But they introduced important technical and horticultural skills, for example, how to grow new crops such as wheat and barley. Rev John Butler recorded in his journals (published as *Earliest New Zealand*) that on 3 May 1820, 'the agricultural plough was for the first time put into the land of New Zealand at Kideekidee [Kerikeri] … I trust that this day will be remembered with gratitude, and its anniversary kept by ages yet unborn.'

They also brought literacy, opening schools, importing printing presses and putting spoken Māori onto the page. Thomas Kendall produced an outline of the Māori language in 1820, William Colenso printed the first Māori translations from the Bible in 1835 and William Williams created the first Māori to English dictionary, printed in 1844 with later editions updated by members of the Williams family.

Samuel Marsden arrives in New Zealand, Christmas Day, 1814.

National Library of Australia

'BRITAIN OF THE SOUTH'

Visitors were ready to praise any similarities to Britain. Charles Darwin described his 1835 visit in *A Naturalist's Voyage Round the World*. At the mission station in Waimate, he was pleased to see 'that happy mixture of pigs and poultry, lying comfortably together, as in every English farmyard'.

New Zealand was often called the *brighter* or *fairer* 'Britain of the South'. The phrase was first used by Joseph Barrow Montefiore who chartered a boat from Australia in 1830 with a view to setting up trading stations here. He thought it was the most beautiful country he had seen, 'a perfect paradise'.

1840S: THE NEW ZEALAND COMPANY

From 1840, and for over a century, the largest proportion of migrants to New Zealand were from Britain: England, Scotland, Ireland and Wales. In the 1840s and early 1850s, many came on assisted passages, with part or all the fare paid, on New Zealand Company ships to its five settlements in Wellington, Nelson, New Plymouth, Otago and Canterbury.

The New Zealand Company, under Edward Gibbon Wakefield, issued its prospectus on 2 May 1839 and its ship the *Tory* left England on 12 May. On board were two of the Wakefields

The New Zealand Company drew up its own constitution and coat of arms (shown here) as it prepared to found its own self-governing settlements in New Zealand.

Archives New Zealand Te Rua Mahara o Te Kāwanatanga

Charles Hursthouse spent several years in New Plymouth. His book *New Zealand, or Zealandia, the Britain of the South* (1857) presented a rosy picture to potential settlers of a fertile land and a safe and comfortable existence.

014872019 The British Library

(William and Edward Jerningham). Their role was to get the settlements ready. The Company needed to move fast if it was to meet its aim of buying land cheaply from Māori to sell on (at a profit) to the settlers before the government took the role of land transfer to itself.

In January 1840, the *Aurora* sailed into Wellington Harbour, bringing the Company's first 148 migrants: married couples, single travellers and children and babies, some born at sea. A few weeks later, on 6 February 1840, Te Tiriti o Waitangi was signed at Waitangi in the Bay of Islands. British migrants arrived with dreams of a better life than the one they were leaving behind. They believed they had bought their land honestly, unaware that the New Zealand Company had sold land it didn't yet own, and that many land sales with Māori would be disputed.

At the same time, as stated in Waitangi Tribunal Report WAI 1040 (2014), Māori rangatira had signed Te Tiriti believing that it seemed to offer them, among other things, 'security from mass immigration and settler aggression'.

The Company's 'Regulations for Labourers Wishing to Emigrate to New Zealand' targeted men who could do the hard work of creating the new colony. Labourers, builders, shepherds, bakers, blacksmiths, boat-builders, carpenters and brickmakers were encouraged to apply for a free passage. Wives travelled for free, as did single women who sailed with parents or relatives or were servants to ladies on board. Children under one year or 15 years and over had a free passage and other children were charged three pounds each.

Wealthier, paying passengers had cabins on deck, but most people were crammed into dark, crowded, rat-infested steerage compartments with little privacy. Storms and seasickness were

LEFT This New Zealand Company share certificate belonged to John Ellerker Boulcott, a director of the Company. He never came to New Zealand, but two of his sons did. Their surname was given to the suburb of Boulcott in Lower Hutt and Boulcott Street in Wellington.

Archives New Zealand Te Rua Mahara o Te Kāwanatanga

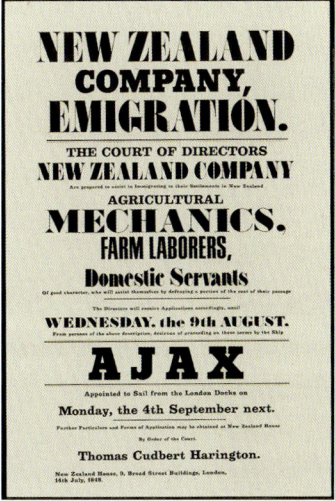

RIGHT New Zealand Company poster from 1848. By this stage, the Company was only offering assisted, not free passages.

LEFT This 1839 New Zealand Company advertisement in the *New Zealand Gazette* invites their preferred settlers to apply for a free passage.

Papers Past, National Library

RIGHT This stamp depicts the first New Zealand Company settlers landing on the beach at Pito-one (Petone) in 1840. It was issued for the 1940 Centennial of New Zealand as a British colony.

Archives New Zealand Te Rua Mahara o Te Kāwanatanga

common; fire, shipwreck and outbreaks of disease were an ever-present risk; even icebergs could be a hazard in the Southern Ocean. The journey took months but music, concerts, dancing, games and church services helped to fill up the time, and there were highlights such as 'Crossing the Line' (a light-hearted ceremony to mark crossing the Equator), spotting whales, dolphins and albatrosses and passing other ships, with the chance of sending mail home.

A young girl who sailed with her family on the *Charlotte Jane* in 1875 remembered, years later, how some of the women burst into tears when their ship finally reached Lyttelton. 'They were crying … because they had all dressed themselves in their Sunday best, and there was nowhere to go.' (*Press*, 9 April 1938) Many migrants were daunted by the rough settlements and harsh conditions but couldn't afford the return fare or risk another sea journey, alarmed by stories of shipwreck, ships vanishing at sea or the horrific fate of the *Cospatrick* which caught fire in 1874 — only 3 out of 473 on board survived. Settlers would never see family and friends again and could only keep in touch by letters that were months old by the time they were delivered.

The Parkhurst boys

Unlike Australia, New Zealand never had convict labour, so when the Parkhurst boys arrived from England in 1842 and 1843, they were met with suspicion and alarm. These boys were convicted for often trivial crimes and sent to Parkhurst Prison on the Isle of Wight to be trained in trades. A total of 128 boys, aged 12 to 20, were sent to New Zealand to find jobs or apprenticeships. It wasn't easy to find people who would hire them, but gradually they settled into jobs or moved elsewhere. Hundreds of Parkhurst boys went to Australia between 1842 and 1852, but no more arrived in New Zealand.

Parkhurst Boys Prison, Isle of Wight.
Illustrated London News, 1847

SOLDIERS AND SURVEYORS

Thousands of British soldiers served in the New Zealand Wars between 1845 and 1870. Some brought wives and children with them. When the regiments left, about one in five stayed on as soldier-settlers. The Fencibles, retired British soldiers, came out by ship with their families between 1847 and 1852 and settled in Auckland in the small villages of Onehunga, Howick, Panmure and Ōtāhuhu. They were promised food, pay and a cottage and land, in return for being a defence force, if needed. (They were only called out once, for a false alarm.) Military settlers, some recruited from the goldfields here and in Australia, were given confiscated Māori land in the 1860s as another way of protecting European communities.

Newspaper advertisement about free and assisted passages, from 1873. Single women were in high demand in the new colony, both as domestic servants and as potential wives.

Papers Past, National Library

It was the job of the surveyors to map out land for the new arrivals. This was a tough job that meant working and camping outdoors in unpredictable weather. Surveyors were heavily dependent on Māori guides for their bush lore and knowledge of local routes and tribes. As they planned the layout of new settlements, the surveyors often chose new names that replaced existing ones. Naming places after people or places they knew was a way to make the British settlers feel more at home.

1870S: JULIUS VOGEL'S PUBLIC WORKS AND IMMIGRATION SCHEME

Assisted passages were also offered by the Plymouth Company, the Otago Association, the Canterbury Association and the six provincial

ABOVE This poster, around 1912, portrays domestic service as a genteel and appealing occupation.

Ref: Eph-A-IMMIGRATION-1912-01-cover, Alexander Turnbull Library, Wellington

TOP Survey camp, Waimate Plains, Taranaki, late 1870s.

Ref: PA1-q-028-33, Alexander Turnbull Library, Wellington

governments (until they were abolished in 1875). The 1870s brought more assisted migrants under Julius Vogel's public works and immigration scheme. As Colonial Treasurer, Vogel planned to boost the economy by borrowing staggeringly large amounts of money from Britain to spend on immigration, buying Māori land and public works projects such as building roads, railways and bridges and extending telegraph lines.

Vogel argued that New Zealand's 'peculiar' shape meant that 'you cannot bring together the two ends nearer than they are. There will always be a certain amount of isolation in different parts until the iron horse runs through the two islands.' (Parliamentary debates, 15 July 1869) Māori had their own trails through the interior but for Europeans, most travel was restricted to the coast. Tracks through the bush were too rough and river crossings often proved fatal. Vogel believed new roads and railways would improve communications and open up inland districts to settlers. The New Zealand Wars were almost over and he claimed that opening up the country for settlement, the arrival of more European immigrants and providing jobs for Māori on public works 'will do more to put an end to hostilities and to confirm peaceful relations, than an army of ten thousand men.' (Parliamentary debates, 28 June 1870)

During debates on the Works Loan Bill (5 September 1870), some MPs spoke against the 'unprecedented grandeur' of the scheme and the size of the loans, but Vogel was undeterred. He called it 'a machinery for colonising work — for the construction of railways and the introduction of immigrants.'

He added:

> *The Government believe that there are in this country vast and valuable forests, great and varied mineral wealth, teeming fisheries, pastoral lands, and enormous agricultural capabilities. Why should we not say to the over-burdened population of the old country, 'Here is a land rich in all natural resources. We are willing to develop it to the largest extent, if you will come and make it your home'?*

Immigrant cottages in Hamilton, late 1800s.

heritage.hamiltonlibraries.co.nz/objects/27349

The arrival of 100,000 assisted migrants helped take the European population from 256,000 to 490,000 in ten years. Most immigrants were still British or Irish, many from rural areas where they were labourers, farmworkers or tradesmen such as carpenters or blacksmiths. Many came direct, but others arrived here after spending some time in Australia.

An English engineering firm, John Brogden and Sons, had the government contract to supply railway workers. They brought out more than 2000 men, wives and children. Brogden's 'navvies' set to work building railway lines and tunnels with few tools or vehicles apart from pickaxes, shovels and horse-drawn carts. In the decade from 1870 to 1880, the railway network grew from 74 kilometres (all in the South Island, often still known as Middle Island) to nearly 2000 kilometres.

CHANGING THE LANDSCAPE

The landscape was being transformed. Forests were cleared and burned; wetlands and swamps were drained. Flax mills and sawmills processed raw flax and logs. Pastoral farming (raising livestock, not growing crops) would grow into a huge export earner from sales of meat, wool, animal hides and dairy products. In many cases, it was the migrants who arrived at this time who contributed to these changes.

SCANDINAVIAN FORESTERS

In the 1870s, the only way through the impenetrable 'Seventy Mile Bush' in the lower North Island was on narrow tracks or along rivers. The Scandinavian countries of Sweden, Norway and Denmark also have large forests, and their forestry workers were targeted under Julius Vogel's public works scheme. They came here, with fares part-paid and the promise of 40-acre plots of land, to clear the forests between Wellington and Napier.

The first group arrived in 1871 on the *Celaeno*. They sailed on to Foxton and then walked to Palmerston North. More ships followed. There was an outbreak of measles and smallpox on board the *England* and

The Laurvig family of Norsewood, taken in about 1883. Edward and his wife Lena arrived in New Zealand from Norway in 1872. Lena died in 1879, aged 32, while giving birth to her seventh child.

Palmerston North City Library

Niels and Ragnhild Hansen, from Denmark, and their four children outside their newly built house at Whakarongo, near Palmerston North; photo taken around 1895.

Palmerston North City Library

three adults and 13 children died, including a new baby. When the ship reached Wellington in March 1872, the passengers had to go into quarantine on Matiu/Somes Island, after waiting at anchor for the quarantine huts to be built. Their precious possessions were burned on the beach to stop the infection spreading.

Families travelled over the Rimutaka (now Remutaka) Hill, women and girls in wagons, men and boys walking alongside. They settled at the southern end of the bush in the Scandinavian camp at Kōpuaranga, near Mauriceville, where they lived in wooden huts with dirt floors and open windows screened with cloth. Others settled at the northern end in Hawke's Bay. For years, the men and older boys hacked their way through the dense, dark bush. Some people carried lanterns during daytime as well as at night to see the way ahead. Some travellers disappeared without trace.

Wives and children helped with clearing the undergrowth and grew food for sale. The women made lace, spun wool and knitted socks and woollen clothes. As with many new arrivals, their faith was an important part of their culture and the Scandinavians built beautiful churches, such as the Norwegian Methodist Church in Mauriceville.

The names of their settlements recalled their homes: Norsewood, Dannevirke and Mellemskov, or 'heart of the forest' in Danish (now Eketahuna). On 6 December 1872, the *Wellington Independent* reported that 'Norsewood ... has now been in existence only six weeks and the whole line of road for a distance of four miles is lined on both sides with neatly constructed residences, gardens are rapidly shooting up about them [and] bush is falling.' The sawmills produced so much wood for building and railway sleepers that Dannevirke was known as 'Sleeper Town'.

> **Seventy Mile Bush**
>
> The Seventy Mile Bush really was 70 miles (112 km) long and about 40 miles (65 km) wide. Pūkaha National Wildlife Centre, Mt Bruce, contains some of its last remnants. Workers at the southern end called it Forty Mile Bush because it was 40 miles from there to Woodville. Māori called it Te tapere nui a Whatonga, or the great domain of Whatonga, after the early explorer Whatonga who climbed a high mountain and saw the trees stretching away into the distance.

In the 1950s and 1960s, another group of Scandinavians arrived from Finland to work in the new pulp and paper mills at Tokoroa and Kawerau. The Finns brought their knowledge of how these mills worked, as well as other features of their life back home, such as saunas.

DALMATIAN GUM DIGGERS

Dalmatia is a province on the coast of Croatia in southern Europe. Before the Balkan War of the 1990s, it was part of Yugoslavia. Before World War I, it belonged to the vast Austro-Hungarian empire. The first Dalmatians came to New Zealand as sailors on board Austrian ships as early as 1859, but many of those who came later worked as kauri gum diggers.

Kauri forests were decimated for building ships, houses, furniture and railway sleepers. The first load of kauri was exported in 1820 and huge areas of forests had disappeared by 1900, leaving only 400 hectares from an estimated previous 1.2 million hectares. The gum diggers fossicked for gum on and under the ground where the kauri forests had been cleared. Kauri gum is a lump of resin that benefits kauri trees by acting like a natural glue to fix any breaks in bark or branches. It was a valuable export, sent overseas for making varnish and linoleum.

In March 1897, a Royal Commission interviewed storekeepers, gum buyers and exporters, gum diggers and settlers for its report on the kauri gum industry. John Billich arrived after he heard about the gum fields from relatives. He said, 'I am a Dalmatian, and was a farmer there. I have been in New Zealand six years. I went straight to the gum-fields … The reason the Austrians come here is because one of us makes a little money, and he does not put it in the bank; he sends it Home to his people,

Lovre Marinovich with family and friend, West Coast Road, Oratia, Auckland.

DGHS Collection, West Auckland Research Centre, Auckland Libraries who are sometimes in great want of money. Then, others at Home, hearing that a digger in New Zealand has sent Home £10 or £20, thinks that New Zealand must be a good place. He says, "I will go there and get some money too."' (Report and Evidence of the Royal Commission on the Kauri-gum Industry, 1898 Session I, H-12, p. 55)

The Report also raised concerns from other gum diggers and settlers that the 'Austrians' worked over the land so thoroughly there was no chance of anyone else finding gum after them. Another common complaint was that they didn't spend their money here, instead sending much of their earnings to family overseas. The Commission believed they would make 'admirable settlers' if they were given blocks of land, but felt that further immigration should be prevented, 'as the supply of both gum and land is by no means inexhaustible'.

The Kauri Gum Industry Act of 1898 ruled that gum digging licences would only be given to those who met certain criteria. These included anyone 'lawfully engaged in digging for kauri-gum' for at least three months, but an Amendment Act in 1910 restricted this to 'a British subject by birth or by naturalization'. This meant the Dalmatian gum diggers could only work on private land by agreement with the landowner.

In World War I, Dalmatians were treated as enemy aliens and some were interned on Somes Island. Later, many turned to farming, fishing or grape-growing or ran restaurants and fish shops. Dalmatian families founded some of the first wine labels in New Zealand. Dalmatian and Māori often worked together in the gum fields and marriages also occurred.

SCOTTISH SHEPHERDS

South Island landscapes were changed by fire and later by farming. Forests were burned first by Māori and then by European settlers. The landscape became one of tussock and scrub. In the 1850s, thousands of sheep were moved south from Nelson to Canterbury. From 1858 to 1867 the number of sheep in Canterbury increased from under half a million to 2½ million. The landscape changed again with new

The Emigrants, painted by William Allsworth in 1814, shows a wealthy Scottish family, tartan-clad, surrounded by luggage and livestock and ready to set off for New Zealand in the ship sailing in the background.

Purchased 1992 with New Zealand Lottery Grants Board funds, Te Papa Tongarewa

farm homesteads, woolsheds and other station buildings, orchards, shepherds' huts, fences, shelter belts, bridges and the first railway lines. European farmers imported animals to graze the land and exotic grass species to grow as pasture. Animal pests such as rabbits and ferrets were introduced, intentionally or by accident, and some caused huge amounts of damage.

Scottish migrants came to all parts of New Zealand, but especially Otago. Some were shepherds who brought their dogs to help work the sheep as well as to provide company on the vast sheep stations. Newspaper advertisements asked for shepherds 'with good dogs'. Today's farm heading dogs are often border collies, a term which refers back to dogs bred for centuries on the borders of England and Scotland.

James Mackenzie's name endures in the Mackenzie country. It was said that his dog only understood commands in Gaelic, and Mackenzie himself may have had little English. Imprisoned in 1855 after a huge flock of sheep went missing, opinions remain divided as to whether he was a thief or an expert shepherd unfairly framed. Accounts of his trial said that he kept silent until his dog was brought in as evidence, when he was overcome with emotion.

In the eighteenth and nineteenth centuries, many farmers of small landblocks in the Highlands and Islands were forced to leave in the Scottish Highland Clearances. Landowners, who wanted more land for sheep farming, evicted their tenants and even burned down the cottages to make sure they couldn't return. Some moved to Nova Scotia and other places in Canada. Years later, potato blight attacked their crops and once again they faced the prospect of famine and a bitterly cold winter. Rev. Norman McLeod led a group who sailed to Australia in 1851 and then on to New Zealand. About 120 people arrived in Auckland in September 1853, and hundreds more followed from Nova Scotia. They settled in Waipu, where they built houses, cleared land for gardens, ground their own flour and built ships to trade with Auckland.

Some migrants came from the Shetland Islands between Scotland and Norway. They stayed close to the sea here, working on the wharves or as fishermen. Some went as far south as Stewart Island and Campbell Island.

Shetland Island farmers with dog and musical instruments, around 1904. These men had been appointed to manage the farm on Campbell Island.

Ref: 1/4-054553-G, Alexander Turnbull Library, Wellington

PREJUDICE AND DISCRIMINATION

The idea of 'Britain of the South' lingered for years. *Seeing New Zealand: The brighter Britain of the South*, a brochure handed out at the British Empire Exhibition in London in 1924, called New Zealand 'More British than Britain, more loyal than the Crown'. It declared 'non-British elements' were 'so small as to be almost negligible … Sturdy settlers have also come here from Norway, Sweden, Denmark, and other countries of Europe, but not in sufficient numbers to affect the general British character of the population.'

The Scandinavians and some Europeans were accepted as migrants. But there was a clear intention, both in popular opinion and government action, to keep out groups who didn't conform to the 'brighter Britain' model. The brochure noted that 'New Zealanders have taken precautions against any influx of undesirable aliens. The people are strongly determined to keep their country white and law-abiding.'

Indian and Chinese, often described as 'coloured immigrants' or 'Asiatics', were among those 'undesirable aliens'. Non-white people, particularly Chinese, were viewed by many as an inferior race who would affect the morals and living conditions of people in other countries. Gambling, opium smoking and the risk of leprosy were seen as potential threats. Another racist phrase used in the late nineteenth and early twentieth century was the 'yellow peril', which implied the imagined danger of hordes of people from the East invading the West.

PREJUDICE AND DISCRIMINATION

TOP LEFT Newspaper cartoons often reflected public opinion. 'The Peril' in the *Observer* (19 July 1920) shows the threat of a turbaned Indian figure named 'Asiatic influx' looming over a New Zealand city.

Papers Past, National Library

TOP RIGHT Another newspaper cartoon (from *The Free Lance*, 1 December 1920) warning of unstoppable waves of migrants arriving.

Papers Past, National Library

LEFT This cartoon (from *The Free Lance*, 9 June 1920) suggests that local workers and diggers (or returned soldiers) will be disadvantaged by large numbers of incoming migrants.

Papers Past, National Library

RIGHT Cover of a pamphlet issued by the White New Zealand League in 1926, telling its readers they have a duty to keep the country 'White' for the sake of their children.

White NZ League, Alexander Turnbul Library, Wellington

Haining Street, Wellington, was once the centre of the city's Chinese community, named by them 'Tong yan gaai' or 'Chinese people's street'. In September 1905 Joe Kum Yung was shot and killed in Haining Street by Lionel Terry, a white supremacist who had written a pamphlet opposing non-European immigration and urging the need to throw off the yellow peril.

ANTI-CHINESE LEGISLATION

From the 1870s prejudice against Chinese immigrants is reflected in myriad pieces of anti-Chinese legislation.

Date	Government Action	
October 1871	Committee of Inquiry into Chinese Immigration into NZ	Report showed positive and negative views of Chinese immigrants: Chinese were seen as industrious, frugal, patient, sober and well-behaved and excellent gardeners. They were 'quiet peaceable miners, who work ground that would hardly be looked at by Europeans, and manage to make a living out of it'.
		However, one warden on the goldfields at Naseby (South Island) said, 'They are by no means to be desired as colonists' and would 'diminish the chances of New Zealand realising the dreams of those who expect her to become the Great Britain of the South'.
		The Committee concluded that the Chinese miners posed no risk to the community and there was no need for any 'legislative action' to exclude them or impose special burdens upon them. This didn't stop a stream of anti-Chinese legislation over following years.
1881	Gaming and Lotteries Act 1881	Made Chinese games of chance (like fantan and pakapoo) illegal.
	Chinese Immigrants Act 1881	Introduction of a poll tax of £10 per person and a tonnage requirement for new arrivals, set at one Chinese passenger per 10 tons of ships' tonnage. By 1896 the ratio was one passenger per 200 tons and the tax was £100.
1898	Shearers' Accommodation Act 1898	Required separate sleeping accommodation for Chinese shearers.
1904, 1910	Shops and Offices Act 1904 and Factories Amendment Act 1910	The Shops Act set opening hours of 8 a.m. to 6 p.m. on weekdays (with one late night a week); the Factories Act specified opening times for laundries. There was a common belief that Chinese gained unfair advantage by working the long hours they were used to in their homeland. They were sometimes fined for working on Sundays; not coming from a Christian background they weren't used to the concept of keeping Sunday as a 'day of rest'.

PREJUDICE AND DISCRIMINATION

Date	Government Action	
1907	Chinese Immigrants Amendment Act 1907	Imposed a tougher entry test. Chinese had to 'read a printed passage of not less than one hundred words of the English language'. From 1910, if Chinese migrants couldn't pass the reading test and other requirements of the Act they were liable for deportation.
From 1908 until 1951	Naturalisation law	Unless they were already naturalised, or were New Zealand born, Chinese were prohibited from becoming naturalised. They could not become citizens, vote, take certain public roles, serve on a jury or join the armed forces. Search warrants weren't needed for police searching Chinese homes for opium.
1934	Temporary lifting of poll tax	
1944	Poll tax formally cancelled	Walter Nash remarked, 'We have no more right to ask the Chinese to pay a poll-tax than we have to ask the Japanese, the Germans, the Spaniards, or the Norwegians,' calling the tax a 'blot on our legislation'.
12 February 2002	PM Helen Clark gives official government apology delivered in English and Mandarin	In her address to Chinese New Year Celebrations, Prime Minister Helen Clark apologised on behalf of the government for the 'considerable hardship' imposed by the poll tax and the way it split families apart. 'Today we also express our sorrow and regret that such practices were once considered appropriate,' she said. 'While the governments which passed these laws acted in a manner which was lawful at the time, their actions are seen by us today as unacceptable. We believe this act of reconciliation is required to ensure that full closure can be reached on this chapter in our nation's history.'
13 February 2023	Official government apology in Cantonese	At the 2023 Chinese New Year Celebration, the government re-issued this apology in Cantonese, the language spoken by the first Chinese migrants.

THE PERMIT SYSTEM

The Immigration Restriction Amendment Act 1920 marked a major change in policy by introducing the permit system. This Act was chiefly aimed at restricting Asian immigration but was also used to apply to other non-British groups. It formed the basis of an unwritten 'White New Zealand' policy that remained in force until the immigration changes of 1987.

Under this Act, 'no person other than a person of British birth and parentage' could enter the country without a permit.

Poll tax certificate for Young Yee Fong (1922).

Ref: MS-Papers-7724, Alexander Turnbull Library, Wellington

On the Bill's second reading on 14 September 1920, Labour leader Harry Holland encouraged his fellow MPs to remember 'that the world is a very small place, and that, biologically speaking, the same red blood of humanity flows in the veins of all of us, no matter what piece of land we happened to be born upon'. But he still supported the Bill for the sake of protecting the standard of living of New Zealand workers.

OTHER LEGISLATION

The Immigration Restriction Act 1899 introduced a language test for 'any person other than of British (including Irish) birth and parentage'. These migrants had to write out and sign their application 'in any European language'. It was a policy designed to weed out people of particular races but disguised as an educational, not a racial test. The usual application was printed at the end of the Act, which meant it could be memorised.

The Old Age Pensions Act 1898 was a triumph for New Zealand social history but excluded 'Chinese or other Asiatic, whether naturalised or not'. (They were also excluded from the Widows' Pension Act 1911 and the Family Allowances Act 1926.) This exclusion was not lifted until 1936.

The 1929 Select Committee on 'Employment of Maoris on Market Gardens' listed examples of Māori women married to, living with or having children with Chinese or Indian men. The Committee noted that 'as a general principle it is not in the

Joala Singh Belling, a Sikh hawker, around 1920.
Ref: 1/2-052817-F, Alexander Turnbull Library, Wellington

interests of public morality that the employment of Maori girls and women by Chinese and Hindus should be permitted to take place', but these were often the only jobs available, so banning the women from working in the gardens 'would in many cases result in hardship'. (*Appendix to the Journals of the House of Representatives, 1929 Session I, G-11*)

Legislation pre-1920 was often aimed at Chinese, but other unwanted groups were also targeted, as seen by the Kauri Gum Industry Act 1898 and later Acts which made it harder for Dalmatians to work as gum diggers. Hawkers were a group of people who carried goods around the country for sale, often on foot. Many were Lebanese, Syrian or Indians (usually referred to as Hindus). Most were men, but not all; Lebanese woman Saada Bacos travelled around Central Otago pushing a large pram full of suitcases of clothing, sewing items and jewellery. The Undesirable Hawkers Protection Act 1896 required hawkers to buy an annual licence, only available to those who were British subjects, naturalised or had lived in the country for 12 months and could provide a certificate of character signed by at least four ratepayers. In Parliamentary debates, Premier Richard Seddon said the country was 'simply deluged' with a class of hawkers who weren't respectable or desirable.

ALIENS

'Aliens' were another targeted group. On 16 November 1840, New Zealand became a separate British colony, no longer linked to New South Wales. People living here were either British citizens, which included Māori and those who were born here, or 'aliens' who could only gain British citizenship by being naturalised.

The Registration of Aliens Act 1917 was passed during World War I. Anyone in the 'alien' category had to register by 1 December 1917, giving details such as name, nationality, place of birth, age, address and date of arrival. The *Press* of 23 November 1917 reported that 'scores of aliens' had registered at the Christchurch police station. 'People of all countries, Russians, Italians,

Scandinavians, Spaniards, Dutch, Chinese, Assyrians, Greeks, and other nationalities too numerous to mention, including a large number of Americans, have hastened to comply with the regulations.' The term 'alien' was finally removed from official use by the Citizenship Act 1977.

Under the Undesirable Immigrants Exclusion Act 1919, nobody from former enemy countries Germany or Austria could land without a licence issued by the attorney-general. Other 'undesirable' immigrants included those who were 'disaffected or disloyal' or whose presence might threaten the 'peace, order, and good government' of the country, a category which reflected concern about socialists and Marxists following the Bolshevik Revolution. People could be deported under this Act. The Immigration Restriction Amendment Act 1931 (passed during the Depression years) set more restrictions 'on account of any economic or financial conditions' that would prohibit the arrival of persons of any 'nationality, race, class, or occupation'.

The Aliens Act required that 'every alien' obtain a certificate of registration.

EPH-PW-1-107, Tāmaki Paenga Hira Auckland War Memorial Museum

THE DISABLED

Although illness, disease and accidents were common in the nineteenth century, there were few organisations to care for the disabled, who mostly relied on family support and church charities, and they made up another group of unwanted migrants. The Imbecile Passengers Act 1882 required a bond of £100 for any passenger, 'lunatic, idiotic, deaf, dumb, blind, or infirm, and likely … to become a charge upon the public or upon any public or charitable institution'. The Immigration Restriction Act 1899 made it unlawful for 'prohibited immigrants' (including anyone who was an 'idiot' or 'insane') to land.

However, public attitudes changed in the aftermath of World War I. The return of soldiers with mental and physical disabilities, and outbreaks of epidemics such as tuberculosis and polio, showed that disability could affect anyone, and more effort was put into rehabilitation and new methods of care. New Zealand was one of the first countries to accept refugees who were (then termed) 'handicapped'. Fifteen families, each with at least one 'handicapped' member, arrived in Wellington from refugee camps in Austria in April 1959.

In 1973, the government agreed that the country's intake of Ugandan Asian refugees would also include 'handicapped' cases: 'Mr Kirk said New Zealand should not say it wanted only "the best apples in the barrel". He was sure most New Zealanders would agree that these were the people who needed help most.' (*Evening Post*, 17 April 1973)

THE WHITE NEW ZEALAND LEAGUE

Indians and Chinese worked (with Māori) in the market gardens in Pukekohe. Their numbers were still small, but local feeling against them ran hot. A group of 60 Pukekohe residents, many of them farmers, voted in 1925 to form the White New Zealand League. Deputy Mayor George Parvin claimed that 'their mode of living was such that a white man could not hope to compete with them. In a short time they would overrun the country.'

The League printed booklets and campaigned to make it illegal for landowners to sell or lease land to Indian or Chinese people. In 1926, the New Zealand Indian Central Association was formed to protest against the League's propaganda and combat discriminatory immigration policies. In the end, the League's support and funds dried up and it petered out in the 1930s.

MORE 19TH-CENTURY ARRIVALS

CHINESE MIGRANTS

Wong Ah Poo Hoc Ting was the first Chinese man to arrive in New Zealand. He was a child when he left his village to work as a cabin boy on sailing ships. In 1842, in his twenties, he was a steward on a ship that came to Nelson, where he went ashore and hid until his ship left. Later he changed his name to Appo Hocton. He was naturalised,

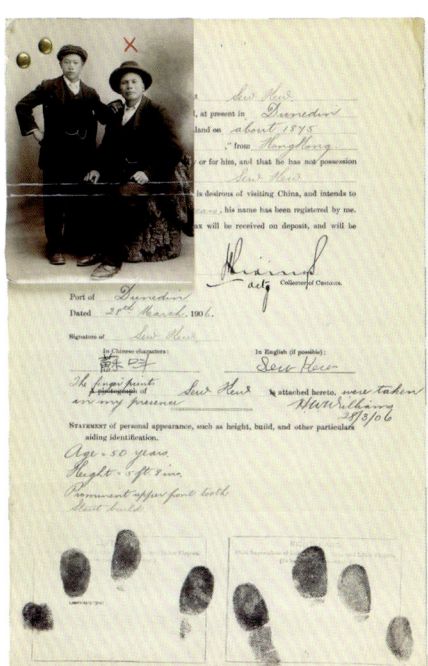 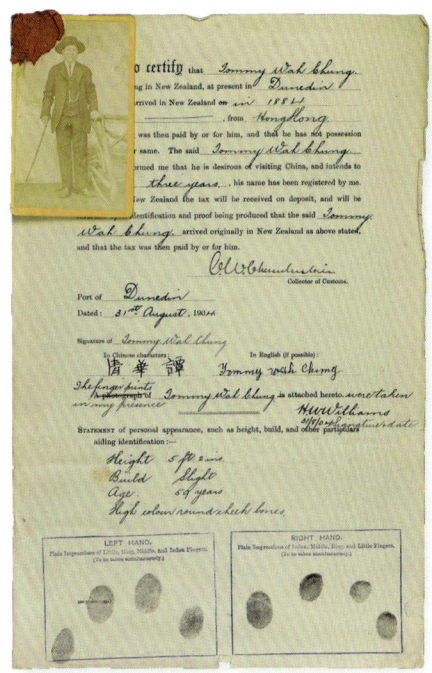

LEFT Sew Key and son. RIGHT Tommy Wah Chung. Chinese immigrants who wanted to leave New Zealand temporarily needed a certificate of registration to allow them to re-enter the country. These images were taken between 1904 and 1956.

DADF/D429/19064/2e; DADF/D429/19064/1k, Archives New Zealand Te Rua Mahara o Te Kāwanatanga

Chew Chong was a successful businessman in Taranaki. The figure at the door of Chew Chong's General Store, New Plymouth, is probably him (c. 1875).

PH02002-406, photographer William Andrews Collis, Puke Ariki

bought land, got married, had children and died in 1920, aged over 100. (Chinese names have the surname placed first, but Chinese often changed their names, or had them changed by customs officials, to match the European pattern and make them easier for Europeans to pronounce.)

Chinese came to work in the goldfields of Central Otago in response to an invitation from the Dunedin Chamber of Commerce who were concerned that the local economy was suffering as gold miners flocked to the newly discovered West Coast gold fields instead.

The Chinese miners called New Zealand 'Sun Gum Shan' (in Cantonese) or 'New Gold Mountain'. Most came from villages in the same part of south-east China: the Pearl River Delta region of Guangdong province, near Canton City (now Guangzhou). They worked hard and sent money back home to support their families, clans and villages. Younger family members were sometimes sent out to join someone who was already working here. The 1871 Committee of Inquiry into Chinese Immigration estimated there were 4215 Chinese in New Zealand, most of them (3570) miners; the next most common occupations were storekeepers and gardeners.

The appearance of these early Chinese immigrants set them apart; they dressed differently and men still wore a queue (where hair is shaved at the front and plaited at the back). They were called 'Orientals' or 'Celestials' from the 'Flowery Land'; pranksters pulled up vegetables in their gardens and threw stones on their roofs or bricks through their windows.

As the gold ran out, many returned to China but some moved into other areas of work, such as market gardening, running fruit shops and laundries; others were rabbiters, hawkers and farm cooks. Successful entrepreneurs included Choie Sew Hoy, who had a gold-dredging company and a store in Dunedin, and Chew Chong, who owned stores and butter factories in Taranaki and exported a fungus that was highly valued in China. It was a male-dominated community; the 1881 census recorded 4995 Chinese males and only 9 females.

Chinese gold miners seated in front of a stone cottage in Central Otago, late 1860s.

Ref: 1/4-009945-G. Alexander Turnbull Library, Wellington

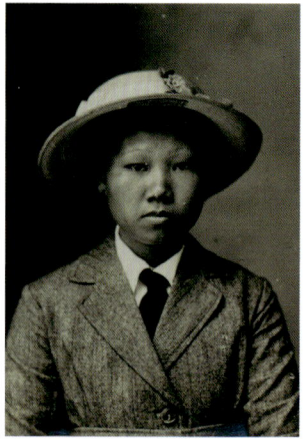

Yee Jack Gin was born in Canton (now Guangzhou) and arrived in New Zealand, aged 19, in 1921. She paid a poll tax of £100.

Archives New Zealand Te Rua Mahara o Te Kāwanatanga

WAR TIME

About 55 New Zealand-born Chinese served in World War I. Victor Low, an engineering student, signed up in 1917; after the war and awaiting passage home from England he had the job of surveying the giant Bulford Kiwi, still visible today, which the soldiers then carved into the hillside. Low's mother, Matilda Lo Keong, is thought to have been the country's first Chinese female immigrant. Racist and anti-Chinese attitudes continued after World War I. Despite this, some Chinese New Zealanders also served in World War II and other conflicts. In 2021, a memorial to the Chinese Anzacs was unveiled at the Lawrence Chinese Camp, Otago.

In October 1938, when the Japanese invaded the Pearl River Delta to try and prevent China from importing arms and supplies, the home villages of Chinese men in New Zealand

Wong Gar Sui, his wife Mew Yuen and three children in W. Chong's fruit shop, 1922.

Ref: 1/2-037502-G, Alexander Turnbull Library, Wellington

came attack. The Chinese community lobbied the New Zealand government to allow their families to join them and this was agreed, based on paying a bond and deposit (of approximately $75,000 in today's money) and an assurance that any children born here would return to China. After subsequent lobbying from the Chinese community and the Presbyterian church it was agreed in 1947 that the families could stay. It was from this point that the Chinese community, which until then had been largely male, began to grow and develop. Chinese market gardeners played an important role in the war effort at home, supplying most of the green vegetables when the government needed huge quantities of food to feed American troops here and in the Pacific.

SS Ventnor

Many Chinese miners saw themselves as temporary residents who intended to return home. If they died here, it was important that their bodies be returned to their families to carry out the traditional ancestral rites so their spirits would be peaceful and happy. The Chinese community enabled this to happen by organising teams of men to dig up the remains from cemeteries under official supervision. The bones were packed in zinc-lined boxes and coffins that were sealed and put on board ship.

Telegram from George Martin, Coastwaiter, Hokianga, reporting on the loss of the SS *Ventnor*.
Archives New Zealand Te Rua Mahara o te Kāwanatanga

In 1883, the SS *Hoihow* successfully returned the remains of 230 men to their families. In 1902, the SS *Ventnor* collected 499 coffins from Dunedin, Greymouth and Wellington. The *Ventnor* set off for Hong Kong but hit a reef off the Hokianga Harbour and sank on 28 October. Thirteen crew and passengers died, including the captain and some old Chinese men who were on board to look after the remains, and most of the coffins were lost.

In the days and months following, some of the bones washed ashore. Those who lived along the coast, including Te Roroa and Te Rarawa iwi, carefully gathered the kōiwi (skeletal remains) and looked after them. Over a century later, Chinese descendants travelled to Hokianga to pay their respects to their ancestors and to thank local iwi for caring for the remains. There are several memorials to the sinking. The wreck of SS *Ventnor* was found in 2014 and is a protected archaeological site under the care of Heritage New Zealand Pouhere Taonga.

INDIAN MIGRANTS

Indian lascars (sailors) travelled the world in the eighteenth and nineteenth centuries. The first Indians to arrive in New Zealand joined the *Saint Jean Baptiste* as crew when it stopped at Pondicherry in India. On 17 December 1769, Captain de Surville landed in Doubtless Bay in search of fresh food and water, and Mahmud Qasim and Nasrin, the two young Indian men, came ashore. Sadly, both died from scurvy later in the journey.

A small Indian community grew up in Christchurch when John Cracoft Wilson, later an MP, moved there from India in the 1850s. Wilson bought up a large plot of land and named it Cashmere, after the hill station of Kashmir. His Indian and Anglo-Indian workers helped to drain the Cashmere swamp and carried stone for the new cathedral on bullock wagons from the Port Hills. The Old Stone House, built in 1870 as their living quarters, has survived fire

Indians and their luggage being transferred from an island steamer to RMS *Niagara* at Auckland, after failing to pass the education test, around 1914.

AWNZ-19140709-50-1, Auckland Libraries Heritage Collections

and earthquakes and is still in use as a community centre today.

Gabriel Read, an Australian miner, is often cited as the person who found gold in Otāgo in 1861. But an Indian man, Edward Peters, known as 'Black Peter', found gold several years earlier around Tuapeka. Governor-General Sir Anand Satyanand (also of Indian descent) unveiled a memorial at Glenore in 2009 to mark the 150th anniversary of his discovery.

In the 1890s, more Indians started arriving, most of them men from the Gujarat and Punjab areas. They worked as road builders, brickmakers, fruit and vegetable sellers, bottle collectors, hawkers, scrub and gorse cutters, and drain diggers. India was part of the British Empire so they could come here freely, as long as (after the Immigration Restriction Act of 1899) they could write out their immigration application form in a European language, usually English. The British sent many Indians to work in sugarcane and other plantations in Fiji. Some of those workers came here after their time in Fiji was up. There were rumours of cramming schools in Fiji where they could study for the writing test, or it might be that they learnt enough English there to fill or copy out the form.

About 100 Indian New Zealanders enlisted in World War I but the practical difficulties of catering to their vegetarian or halal diets meant that most were turned down. Jagt Singh was wounded at Chunuk Bair in Gallipoli but survived. Ratan Chand Mehra was killed on 3 December 1917, in France.

In the 1920s the Indian population was still small (the 1921 census recorded 1925 in total) but despite being British subjects, they often faced racism and prejudice. In 1920, eight Indian scrub cutters couldn't find anywhere to stay in Masterton. When they found rooms in a boarding house in Carterton instead, local people started a protest outside. The men caught a train back to Masterton and camped in a park before travelling north the next day.

Many early Indian migrants were men whose families stayed in India until they could afford the fare to bring them out. It was hard to find Indian spices and vegetables in New Zealand. Clothing was different and for a long time there was nowhere to buy saris and

> ### The children of Kalimpong
>
> In 1908, the first of a group of 130 Anglo-Indian teenagers came out to New Zealand. These were the children of English tea planters and Indian or Nepalese women. There was prejudice in both England and India against Anglo-Indian children. Rev. John Anderson Graham, a Scottish missionary, set up St Andrew's Colonial Homes in Kalimpong, near Darjeeling, to give these children a safe home. Rev. Graham hoped to find permanent homes for the children in British colonies but New Zealand was the only colony that took them. Siblings followed their older brothers and sisters as they became old enough and they worked for local families as farm labourers (the boys) and domestic help (the girls). The scheme ran for 20 years until 1938.
>
>
>
> The first large group of young people from Kalimpong to arrive in New Zealand, 1912.
>
> Courtesy of National Library of Scotland

women had to rely on friends and family going back to India to buy them. In the book *With a Suitcase of Saris*, children of these brave and resilient Indian women remember how hard they worked, cleaning, cooking, sewing and gardening, often for large families, but there were highlights too: watching Indian movies, visiting other Indian families, Indian weddings and delicious homemade food, pickles, sweets and snacks.

From the 1970s, Indians began purchasing dairies as a way of diversifying from selling fruit and vegetables and becoming more independent. Dairies often became, and remain, important community hubs. The children of migrants became the first generation to attend university, carving out professional careers in medicine, IT and other areas. The 1980s onwards saw another big change when many Fijian Indians came to New Zealand after the Fijian military coups. International students also started to arrive in large numbers. Cultural activities and events began to have a wider and more public outreach, from floats on Christmas parades to Diwali celebrations.

GERMAN MIGRANTS

The first group of German migrants arrived in Nelson on the *St Pauli* on 14 June 1843, nearly six months after leaving Hamburg. The next year, more families and single adults arrived on the *Skiold*. They were farmers, blacksmiths, carpenters, cobblers, butchers, weavers, artists, musicians, wine makers, fruit growers, saw millers, hop and tobacco growers, church ministers, missionaries and scientists.

The German migrants settled in places such as Germantown in Southland, Hanover Valley in Canterbury and Ranzau, St Paulidorf, Neudorf, Rosental and Sarau near Nelson. The land was rough, bush-covered or swampy and it was hard work cutting trees and building roads, churches and schools. Settlers in the Bohemian settlement of Pūhoi, north Auckland, found their new home surrounded not by the pasture and farmland they were expecting, but buried in the middle of dark and dense kauri and totara forest. They had no money to go anywhere else and without the help of Ngāti Rongo, they might not have survived.

For many years, there were more immigrants

SPECIAL ADVERTISEMENTS.

A DISCLAIMER.

A REPORT has been circulated that I am of German origin. It is not true, which I can prove. Both my parents were English. I was born in Shropshire, England, where my father and grandfather were born, and neither were ever out of England and Wales until a few years back. My ancestors lived on the same farm for 600 years. I have at least six relatives in France fighting against the Germans, and one in Egypt. I have been in New Zealand 35 years. If anyone can prove that I have any German blood, or sympathised with the Germans in any way, I will give £50 to the New Zealand Hospital Ship. I would rather die than come under German rule, and sincerely hope that when they are beaten they will be so crushed that they cannot rise again.

E. BACH.

Strong anti-German feeling during World War I prompted some people with foreign-sounding surnames to place newspaper advertisements stating that they weren't German.

Papers Past, National Library; *The Hawera & Normanby Star*, 22 May 1915

German soldiers on Somes Island, 1917.
Ref: 1/2-112229-F, Alexander Turnbull Library, Wellington

from Germany than from anywhere else apart from Britain, but when war broke out in 1914, German-born people were classed as enemy aliens, even if naturalised. Some New Zealand-born Germans joined up, knowing that they might be fighting against relatives, and the Women's Anti-German League asked the Defence Department to check the loyalty of soldiers with German-sounding surnames. People broke windows of German-owned shops, boycotted German businesses and accused German neighbours of being spies and passing information to ships by signalling at night with lights.

Hostile anti-German feeling led to place names being changed. Sarau (named after a village in Germany) became Upper Moutere. Some people changed their surnames or placed notices in the newspapers to prove they didn't come from Germany. Lutheran churches in the

Manawatu settlements of Rongotea and Halcombe were burned down.

The government interned over 500 Germans on Somes Island in Wellington Harbour and about 70 on Motuihe Island in the Hauraki Gulf. These included ships' crews, a touring brass band and German officials from Samoa, as well as men who had lived here for years. The most famous was Count Felix von Luckner who made a daring escape from Motuihe Island in December 1917. He and his men were free for a week before being recaptured.

The internees on Somes Island had to work hard and were often badly treated by the guards. When the war ended, they were moved to Featherston camp so the island could be used as a quarantine station for returning troops. In May 1919, the government put 410 internees on board the *Willochra* and sent them back to Germany.

In World War II, some Germans were again interned on Somes Island. The Aliens Committee was set up to sort 'enemy aliens' into different classes according to how much danger they posed to the state. Even if not interned, people in this category had to register with the police and report if they changed address or went away from home for more than a day. They couldn't own firearms, large-scale maps, nautical charts, radios with short wave reception or cameras without a special police permit, and many cameras were confiscated.

More Germans arrived from the 1990s on, attracted by New Zealand's clean green image. Today there are thousands of people in New Zealand with German ancestry.

IN THE SHADOW OF WAR

JEWISH AND WAR-TIME REFUGEES

In the 1930s, about 1100 migrants arrived from Germany, Austria, Czechoslovakia, Poland and Hungary. Some were Jewish, or married to Jewish people, or opposed the regime of Nazi Germany. They were desperate to escape, but it was hard to find any country that would take them. To get into New Zealand under the 1920 Immigration Restriction Act they needed an entry permit and these were not easy to obtain, even for those with money; often it came down to chance, luck and knowing the right people, such as relatives already here or other New Zealand citizens who could act as guarantors.

These newcomers from Central Europe were often seen as being 'different'. They bowed, hugged and kissed when greeting each other and spoke loudly with impassioned gestures. No matter how good their English was, their accents showed that they came from somewhere else. Used to big, sophisticated cities with historic buildings and a rich cultural life, they, in turn, found everything different here: language, food, weather, the wooden houses spread over the hills. They missed familiar food: yoghurt, cottage cheese, rye bread, salami, coffee and favourite cakes, and were delighted when the first coffee houses opened, giving them venues to meet in.

The wartime escapees felt lucky and grateful to be in New Zealand but carried the weight of all they had lost. They left behind jobs, houses, beloved family and friends and precious possessions, and could never go back because their old lives had been destroyed by

Polish refugee children boarding a train to Pahiatua, on wharves at Wellington, November 1944.

Pascoe, John Dobree, 1908–72. Ref: 1/2-003647-F. Alexander Turnbull Library, Wellington

war and Nazism. Many were professors, teachers, lawyers or doctors, but they struggled to find jobs.

After the war, more people arrived from Central Europe, both relatives and refugees. The Central European migrants included philosophers, scholars, artists, photographers, writers, poets, dancers, musicians, craftspeople, architects and designers who would make a big impact on the cultural life of New Zealand. Karl Popper, Ernst Plischke, Marie Blaschke, Maria Dronke, Sir Thomas Eichelbaum, Fred Turnovsky, Peter Munz and Friedensreich Hundertwasser all became well known in their chosen fields.

THE POLISH CHILDREN

During World War II the German army under Adolf Hitler tried to invade the Soviet Union. This forced the Soviet Union to join the Allies, including Britain and Poland, who were all now fighting a common enemy. Polish prisoners who had been held in Russia were set free but couldn't return home because Poland was in the middle of a war zone. Instead they travelled south to Uzbekistan (where the Polish army was gathering), by train, on carts, on foot or even by camel, in ragged clothes and shoes that were falling apart, selling their last possessions to buy food on the way.

Many of the children had become orphans or were separated from their families and were moved to Isfahan, Iran. One group of

Polish refugees on their way to the Polish Children's Camp at Pahiatua, 1944.

Archives New Zealand Te Rua Mahara o Te Kāwanatanga

children were offered a new home in Mexico. On the way, their ship stopped at Wellington where Countess Maria Wodzicka, wife of the Polish Consul, met Janet Fraser, wife of Prime Minister Peter Fraser, who persuaded her husband to invite a group of children to New Zealand.

The Polish children left Iran in October 1944 for a land they knew little about, except that it was green and beautiful. There were 733 of them, from toddlers to teenagers, and 105 adults, mostly teachers and caregivers. In Bombay (now Mumbai), they transferred to an American troopship, the USS *General Randall*, which sailed into Wellington Harbour on 31 October 1944 and docked the next day. The children and adults were met on board by the prime minister and then put on trains that took them to Pahiatua railway station from where they travelled on to what became known as the Polish Children's Camp, nicknamed Little Poland. There were separate dormitories for boys and girls, a school, a chapel, laundries and gardens. People had donated toys, books and clothes, and women from the Polish Children's Hospitality Committee made up the beds and decorated the rooms with flowers.

The children were taught in Polish and celebrated Polish festivals, because they expected to go back to Poland. But when World War II ended, Poland was under Soviet communist rule. It was too dangerous to return, and many had no family or home to return to, so the New Zealand government allowed them to stay. They left the camp as they got older to attend secondary schools or boarding schools or go to work. There were hostels for working-age young people, such as the Polish Girls' Hostel in Lyall Bay and Polish Boys' Hostel in Island Bay, Wellington.

The last children left the camp in April 1949, but many of the boys and girls who lived there retained a special bond for the rest of their lives and a number of them later married each other. A sculpture by Tanya Ashken, representing a mother and child, marks where the camp used to be, and a plaque on the Wellington waterfront commemorates their arrival in 1944.

BRITISH CHILD MIGRANTS

From the 1860s, and especially in the years before and after World War II, thousands of children were sent from Britain overseas under the Child Migrant programme. Between 1948 and 1954, about 600 child migrants, some only five or six years old, came to New Zealand.

Some children were placed in orphanages because both parents had died or a solo parent couldn't manage alone. Other families were poor or homeless and believed their children would have more opportunities in another country. Many children like this were put on a ship with a suitcase of clothes and sent to the other side of the world.

In New Zealand, most children were placed in foster homes,

Young British immigrants, aged from 5 to 15, arriving in Wellington, 4 October 1940.

Ref: PAColl-5482-022, The *Dominion Post* Collection, Alexander Turnbull Library, Wellington

but these were not always permanent. Some children were moved around a lot; some were well treated, others less so. They lost touch with their families in England, or only found them again years later. In 2009, the Australian government apologised to former child migrants for how they were treated, and the British government did the same in 2010.

CHINESE ORPHANS

In the 1950s and 1960s refugees fleeing communist China and famine flocked into Hong Kong. Some Chinese babies were sent from Hong Kong orphanages to new families overseas, including to New Zealand. The first ten, baby girls aged between one and three, arrived in Wellington in January 1963 under a government-approved programme organised by the National Council of Churches and other church groups. They were accompanied by two

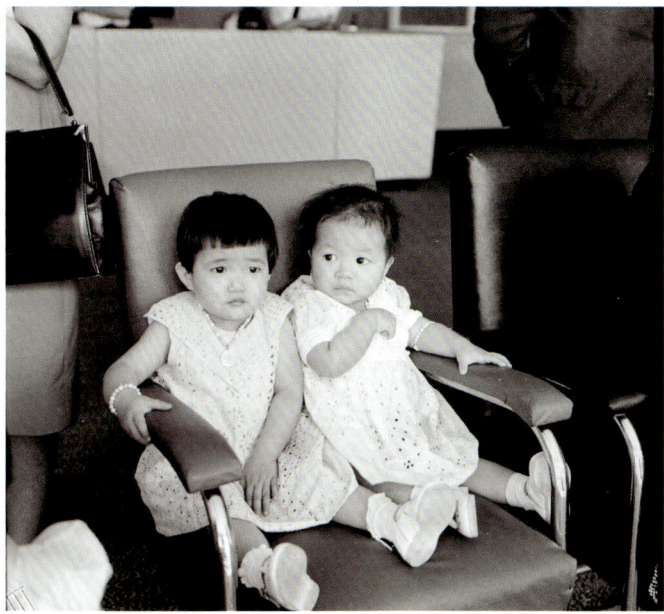

Chinese orphan girls from Hong Kong. The girls were among a group of ten children who arrived at Wellington Airport on 4 January 1963. All of them had adoptive parents waiting in New Zealand.

Ref: EP/1963/0026/F, The Dominion Post Collection, Alexander Turnbull Library, Wellington

caregivers and fussed over during the flight by the air stewards and hostesses, but knowing no English, and used to different food, they must have felt confused and overwhelmed. More than 100 parents applied to adopt the 50 babies who came under this scheme.

WAR BRIDES

'War brides' met New Zealand soldiers serving overseas and moved with them back to New Zealand. During World War II, these future wives and husbands met in England, France, Italy, Greece and Japan. They met on trains, buses and railway stations, at dances, in hospitals or at soldiers' clubs where women volunteered to help out. In Italy and Greece, they met in villages that hid and sheltered New Zealand soldiers.

Some couples got married only weeks after meeting. Brides wore borrowed wedding dresses and veils, or dresses made from parachute silk, or family and friends donated their clothing vouchers to buy something new.

The troops returned home when the war ended but most of the fiancées and wives (and children, if they had any) had to wait for special 'bride ships'. They were nicknamed 'Mr Jones' Wives'

War brides, babies and soldiers landing from the *Ruapehu*. There were 185 brides and 80 children on board.

Otago Daily Times, Otago Witness, 5 March 1919.

because Frederick Jones, Minister of Defence, was in charge of their transport. One troopship, the *Rangitata*, was called the 'Stork Ship' because of all the babies on board.

Some war brides were terribly homesick. They had followed their hearts across the world, but that meant leaving their own families behind. Some struggled with a language barrier or faced criticism from people who thought the men should have married local girls. But other families were warm and welcoming and soon many of the war brides were busy with children and their new lives.

COLD WAR REFUGEES

The Cold War began around the end of World War II and lasted until the Soviet Union broke up in 1991. It was a war of threats, suspicion, propaganda and economic actions, with the Soviet Union and United States and their allies lined up on each side.

Hungary was one of the Eastern European countries under the communist rule of the

Soviet Union. The October 1956 Hungarian Revolution started as a student protest march in the capital city, Budapest. When the revolution was quashed by secret police and Russian troops, 200,000 Hungarian people trekked across the borders to Austria or Yugoslavia.

About 1100 Hungarian refugees came to New Zealand. The first ones arrived in Auckland in December 1958 after a four-day flight. At the airport, Junior Red Cross members held up placards in the colours of the Hungarian flag with a message of welcome in Hungarian. The refugees were given sweets, new clothes and a pamphlet with translations of common words, and the next day they were taken sightseeing, including to the beach. Many of them had never seen the sea before.

Another Cold War protest movement was the Prague Spring in August 1968. Prague was then the capital of Czechoslovakia, now of the Czech Republic. Again the Soviet tanks rolled in and people fled over the land borders to escape communist rule. About 125 of these Cold War refugees from Czechoslovakia came to New Zealand.

Hungarian refugees on a bus, Wellington, 1956.

Ref: EP/1956/2937-F, Alexander Turnbull Library, Wellington

NEW OPPORTUNITIES

New opportunities were not just for those arriving from overseas. At this time many Māori began to move from rural areas to the cities, undergoing a change of lifestyle that brought its own challenges.

When assisted migration began again after World War II, the government was keen to see new migrants assimilating, or fitting in to New Zealand society. Free evening classes in English started in 1951. Attendees were given certificates of attendance and told these would be helpful when applying for naturalisation. Booklets such as *Alien to Citizen: A Bulletin for New Settlers* (Dept of Education, 1953) gave guidance about what to expect and how to behave.

TEN POUND POMS

This post-war assisted migrant scheme was aimed mostly at the British, although some people came from the Netherlands and a few other countries. Young, single migrants came to work as miners, sawmillers, builders, farm or factory workers, nurses, hospital kitchen or ward staff, domestic staff — all roles that were short of employees. Others were married with families and keen to move to Australia or New Zealand where there were plenty of jobs and parents thought it would be a healthier place for their children to grow up. Children travelled for free

An emigration poster designed to entice young single men and women to come out to New Zealand, 1949.

Archives New Zealand Te Rua Mahara o Te Kāwanatanga

British children arriving on board the *Rangitata*, October 1940.

Ref: 1/2-123892-G, Alexander Turnbull Library, Wellington

and adults only paid £10, which is where the nickname 'Ten Pound Poms' came from ('pom' was a slang term for British people).

Travelling by ship was a long journey and a big adventure. The children played games on deck while the adults went to dances, talent quests, singalongs and lectures about life in New Zealand. They were allocated a job, which could be anywhere, and had to stay in it for two years or pay their own fare back. Some homesick families did go back, but many stayed. This policy of assisted migration continued until 1975.

AUSTRIA

In the 1950s the government decided to import 500 prefabricated houses from Austria to help combat a housing shortage. They also paid the fares for 190 Austrian skilled tradesmen

Foundations of an Austrian pre-fabricated house.

Ref: 114/344/07-G, The Dominion Post Collection, Alexander Turnbull Library, Wellington

to build them. The houses were built in Titahi Bay, Wellington, and many are still standing. The Austrian builders stayed in huts that American soldiers had lived in during the war. They enjoyed swimming and dances after work and attended English classes and film evenings. Many were keen motorcyclists, so they were given German translations of traffic regulations and road safety information. After the houses were finished, a few of the builders went back home, but most stayed in New Zealand.

ITALY

The first Italian to reach New Zealand was Antonio Ponto, a sailor on Cook's *Endeavour*. Later there were Italian missionaries and Italian gold miners. The miners worked at places such as Italian Gully on the West Coast (South Island) and Garibaldi Diggings near Naseby in Central Otago.

Italian tunnellers working on the Tongariro power project in the 1960s.

Ref: PAColl-7327, Alexander Turnbull Library, Wellington

In the late nineteenth and early twentieth century millions of Italians left home in search of a better life. They scattered across the world to America, Canada, South America, Australia and New Zealand. When they could afford it, they brought their wives and children, or went back to find a wife. Some husbands and wives spent years apart before they were reunited.

Italian men were fishermen, fish shop owners, market gardeners, grape growers and dairy and sheep farmers. Some were musicians who played at parties and concerts and in cinemas for silent movies. Italian street musicians often had pet monkeys and played an instrument called a hurdy gurdy by turning a wheel with a handle on the side. In the 1920s stone workers from northern Italy brought their knowledge of terrazzo, a flooring material made by mixing marble, stone or glass chips into cement, invented in 16th-century Venice as a way of reusing leftover bits of marble.

Italian communities were close-knit and often came together for birthdays, saints' feast days, weddings and celebrations. In Nelson, tomato growers helped each other at times of intensive work, going from one glasshouse to the next.

In Island Bay, Wellington, the Italian community was linked by their work on the fishing boats. Men from a cluster of Italian

Group of fishermen on the beach at Island Bay, Wellington, in the late 1920s.
Ref: 1/2-047910-G, Alexander Turnbull Library, Wellington

> **Chain migration**
>
> The pattern of migration when people from one area emigrate and encourage family and friends to follow is called 'chain migration'. For example, many Italians came from the same parts of Italy (such as Massa Lubrense near Naples and Stromboli, a volcanic island near Sicily) and went to the same parts of New Zealand, such as Nelson, Makara, Eastbourne and Island Bay, known as 'Little Italy'.

families would fish together (such as the Basile, Dellabarca, Famularo, Greco, Muollo, Ruocco and Volpicelli families). They learnt to adjust to the tides, weather and changeable conditions in Cook Strait and off the Wairarapa coast, made their own nets and wove crayfish pots out of cane and supplejack vines. At Christmas, they would walk around the neighbourhood from house to house singing Italian songs to the accompaniment of guitar and mandolins.

Italian families missed familiar foods and were shocked to find that olive oil was only available in small bottles from chemist shops. They planted vegetable gardens to grow capsicum, eggplant and garlic and made their own pasta, mozzarella cheese, salami and tomato sauce. Italian home gardeners were (and still are) proud of their tomatoes, grown from seed that came from Italy. Every year they planted new tomatoes from the previous season's seeds, so the tomatoes formed a link with their homeland.

In World War II, Italy initially sided with Germany, and some Italians were interned on Somes Island. The Italian fishermen in Wellington were allowed to keep working as long as their gear passed police inspection on each trip, but they couldn't sail too near the harbour entrance and their shortwave radios were sealed to stop them transmitting information. After the war more Italians came to New Zealand, including the tunnellers who worked on hydroelectric projects at Manapouri and Turangi in the 1960s.

GREECE

The first Greeks came to New Zealand as gold miners and fishermen. Like the Italians, they helped to pay for family to join them here.

More came after World War II, when it was hard to get jobs in Greece, and on top of the aftermath of war, there was a civil war.

People from the island of Crete have a special bond with New Zealand. During World War II, Cretan villagers fed and sheltered New Zealand soldiers, knowing they might be shot for doing so. Between 1962 and 1964, a group of nearly 300 young Greek women, mostly from Crete, arrived on a government scheme to work as domestic staff in hotels and hospitals. At that time, few Greek women travelled on their own or lived away from family, so this was very unusual. Some of the women later returned home but others married and stayed here. The Greek Orthodox Church in Wellington is on Hania Street, named after the city in Crete.

New Greek immigrants working in the Wellington Hospital laundry, 1963. The women had arrived in New Zealand just the day before.

Ref: EP/1963/0904-F, The Dominion Post Collection, Alexander Turnbull Library, Wellington

THE NETHERLANDS

In June 1939, five young Dutch carpenters arrived in New Zealand. Their first project was to build a scenic railway that took visitors around the Centennial Exhibition in Wellington. After their photos appeared in the newspaper, they were often recognised and even got invited into people's homes. They were followed by others who came as assisted migrants (like the 'Ten Pound Poms') or because they had valuable work skills. In February 1950, a party of 45 Dutch migrants arrived by flying boat from Sydney. They included a bulb grower, florist, cheesemaker, plumber and carpenter, as well as a family with nine children who were going sharemilking.

Some of the men were engaged to girls back home. In 1953, 26 Dutch fiancées came out to

Newly arrived Dutch migrants standing in front of their luggage, Wellington, 1953.

Archives New Zealand Te Rua Mahara o Te Kāwanatanga

join them on a special 'Bride Flight'. Travelling by air (not by ship) was still unusual and this flight took nearly 50 hours from London to Christchurch, with multiple stops on the way.

During World War II, Dutch people were captured by the Japanese in Indonesia and held in prison camps. In 1946, several hundred survivors arrived in New Zealand on the hospital ship *Tasman* with nothing but the ragged clothes they wore. They recuperated at camps such as Camp Oranje in Auckland, run by the Netherlands East Indies Welfare Organisation. A group of 40 orphans had a special playroom with table tennis and games at the Tomahawk army camp in Dunedin. Most of the evacuees returned to their homes, but one said that New Zealand was 'the nearest place to heaven that I have seen. The people of this country are kinder than I had ever dreamed and to see the children smile again almost compensates for the years of imprisonment.' (*Northern Advocate*, 8 March 1946)

MĀORI MIGRATION TO THE CITIES

In the early years of European migration, many iwi developed profitable trading ventures. They built flour mills, operated coastal vessels and supplied goods and produce to towns and other markets. When much of their land was taken, they lost their economic base, and as the 19th century progressed and they were exposed to introduced diseases such as measles, mumps and influenza, their population dived steeply. Many Pākehā believed that Māori would eventually disappear altogether. Dr Isaac Featherston, superintendent of the Wellington province, declared in 1856 that 'The Maoris are dying out and nothing can save them. Our plain duty as good, compassionate colonists is to smooth down their dying pillow. Then history will have nothing to reproach us with.'

This theory was quoted for many years but gradually the Māori population began to increase again. Māori still lived mainly in rural areas, often working in farming, forestry, fishing or mining. By the 1920s and 1930s, it was becoming harder to find work. The land that was left to them was less fertile and not enough to provide jobs for everyone. Māori began moving to the city. During World War II, more went to work in city factories and workplaces for the war effort. After the war, this movement turned into a flood.

The 1936 census showed that 83% of Māori lived in rural areas, but the percentage in rural and urban areas reversed completely over the next fifty years. In 1986, 83% of Māori lived in urban areas. This has been described as one of the fastest rates of urbanisation worldwide. It is often referred to as 'the second great migration'.

Before this, the majority of Māori and Pākehā had lived separate lives. Even the census was carried out separately until 1951. Many Pākehā might never meet Māori, let alone live next door to them. Cities promised better opportunities for Māori, but they had to negotiate the changes involved in moving from their ancestral kāinga to a new urban way of life where they often met

A group of workers on a city building site laying down a hāngi for Christmas in a metal skip filled with earth, December 1974.

Ref: EP/1974/7746/8-F, The Dominion Post Collection, Alexander Turnbull Library, Wellington

The hotel in this article refused to serve Māori.

Auckland Libraries Heritage Collection, newspaper article, 27 February 1952

discrimination in housing, employment and their social life. In the book *The Silent Migration*, Mihipeka Edwards recalled that:

> It was very hard, very embarrassing, trying to get a place to stay. Because I was a Māori they just looked at me and shut the door. They said they were full up (while the vacancy sign was still in the window). You could have the very best job but still no one wanted you to live in their house.

In 1959, Dr Henry Rongomau Bennett was refused a drink in a hotel in Pukekohe because he was Māori, an act of blatant racism that even made headlines in *The New York Times*. Elsewhere in Pukekohe, barbers' shops wouldn't serve Māori customers, Māori were excluded from the best seats in the local cinema and Māori children could only swim in the public pool on Fridays. It wasn't until the Race Relations Act 1971 that actions like these, invoking discrimination by reason of 'colour, race, or ethnic or national origins' were legally banned.

'Pepper potting'

The 1960 Hunn Report into the Department of Maori Affairs concluded that 'the "urban drift" can be welcomed as the quickest and surest way of integrating the two species of New Zealander'. The desired aim of 'integration' was behind the Department of Maori Affairs' policy of 'pepper potting', or dotting houses for Māori

TOP Standard plans for houses built under Department of Maori Affairs housing schemes from the 1930s to 1980s.

Archives New Zealand Te Rua Mahara o te Kāwanatanga

ABOVE RIGHT Māori and Pākehā children outside a brand-new Department of Maori Affairs state house in south Auckland, 1970s.

Archives New Zealand Te Rua Mahara o te Kāwanatanga

amongst Pākehā communities. This was meant to help ease their move into Pākehā society and to soothe Pākehā who were alarmed at having Māori neighbours. (Later the policy was dropped and some suburbs became largely Māori.)

Te Ao Hou, a Māori magazine, printed tips about keeping house and garden tidy and reminded new city dwellers to hang washing on clothes lines, not fences. There were competitions for 'best kept Maori home and garden'. Houses were clearly meant to conform to the Pākehā houses around them.

In 1966, the Department of Maori Affairs published a booklet called *Our Home* that covered topics such as paying a mortgage, rates and insurance, house painting and repairs, and how to be 'friendly and considerate' neighbours by taking pride in the home and its surroundings.

The Māori Hostel movement

In World War II, many young Māori moved to the city to work in essential industries, but it wasn't easy to find suitable accommodation. This was seen as a particular problem for young Māori women. In September 1845, *The White Ribbon* (the magazine of the Women's Christian Temperance Union or WCTU) reported that, 'Girls took rooms in apartment houses, and had to go to cafes for meals … They were just hanging about the street with nowhere to go.'

The WCTU and other organisations opened hostels in Auckland to care for Māori young people, initially for girls and later for boys. From the 1950s, Trade Training Schemes were designed to encourage young Māori men into skilled trades like carpentry, plumbing, painting, welding and mechanics. In 1954, the first group of Māori boys travelled by train and ferry from the East Coast to join the Maori Apprentices Trade Training Scheme in

Hāngi being prepared for the Rehua Māori Boys' hostel annual fair, October 1971.
Christchurch Star Archive, Christchurch City Libraries

The Ngāti Pōneke Club in Wellington provided a space for young Māori who were new to the city to meet and socialise, such as at this dance in the 1950s.

Archives New Zealand Te Rua Mahara o Te Kāwanatanga

Christchurch. They lived in the Rehua Maori Boys Hostel, set up by members of the Wesleyan Church (Hāhi Wēteriana) and Ngāi Tahu. The apprentices helped to build a wharenui (Te Whatu Manawa Maoritanga o Rehua) to represent iwi from around the country. This later became Rehua Marae.

These hostels and new community centres, like the Māori Community Centre in Auckland (founded in 1947) provided spaces for Māori from different iwi to gather and socialise for the first time. In Wellington, the Ngāti Pōneke Young Māori Club was a place of friendship and belonging that helped young people to hold onto their culture. They practised for fundraising concerts and sang on the radio and at military camps, hospitals and welcome home functions for returned servicemen.

PASIFIKA PEOPLES

Pasifika people have come to New Zealand from islands across the Pacific: Cook Islands, Fiji, Kiribati, Niue, Papua New Guinea, Samoa, Solomon Islands, Tokelau, Tonga, Tuvalu and Vanuatu. In 1945, there were fewer than 2200 Pasifika people living in Aotearoa, but through the 1950s and 1960s they were encouraged to fill gaps in the labour market. They came to New Zealand, especially Auckland, to work in factories, agriculture and forestry and hotels. These were often poorly paid and manual jobs. Pasifika people also had to adjust to a cooler climate, bigger cities, different houses and a very different lifestyle.

Today there are over 380,000 Pasifika people in New Zealand, about two-thirds of them living in Auckland. It is a youthful population; the 2018 census recorded that the median age was 23.4 years old. Of the total number, 66.4% were born in New Zealand and 33.6% overseas.

Pasifika people have made their mark in many different areas including the arts, music, writing, theatre, sport and in government. Albert Wendt was the first published Pacific Island novelist with

Tongan and Samoan women working at an Auckland fish factory in 1977.
Archives New Zealand Te Rua Mahara o Te Kāwanatanga

Sons for the Return Home (1973). Other famous names include rugby player Jonah Lomu, artists Fatu Feu'u and John Pule, poets Alistair Te Ariki Campbell, David Eggleton, Selina Tusitala Marsh, Tusiata Avia and Karlo Mila, writers Lani Wendt Young, Sia Figiel and Courtney Sina Meredith, playwright Oscar Kightley and the Naked Samoans, opera trio Sol3 Mio, and comedian Rose Matafeo. In 2023 Carmel Sepuloni, of Samoan, Tongan and New Zealand European descent, was appointed deputy prime minister.

The Dawn Raids

Cook Island, Niue and Tokelau people could enter the country freely as New Zealand citizens. Other Pasifika ethnicities needed a visa that let them stay and work legally for a certain length of time. If they stayed beyond that time, they became overstayers. In the 1970s, the economy slowed and unemployment rose. Between 1974 and 1976, the Labour government and then the National government under Prime Minister Robert Muldoon began a campaign to enforce the laws against overstayers. Police entered factories to check on workers and stopped people on the streets to inspect their visas. They carried out terrifying early morning 'Dawn Raids', with dogs, on houses where overstayers might be living. If their visas had expired, these people could be deported to their home country. There were overstayers from other countries such as Australia, Canada and South Africa, but the Dawn Raids and random street checks concentrated on Pasifika people who were identifiable because of the colour of their skin.

In 1971, the Polynesian Panther Party (PPP) was founded at a meeting in Ponsonby, Auckland. It was a social justice movement based on the American Black Panthers, with the aim of uniting Pasifika people of all backgrounds to fight racism and injustice. The PPP countered the Dawn Raids by staging their own early-morning protests outside the homes of MPs and they set up the Police Investigation Group (or PIG Patrol) to follow police and watch for any incidents unfairly targeting Pasifika or Māori.

The PPP also carried out community work; they set up homework centres and food banks, held concerts at old folks' homes, organised free transport for people to visit family members and friends in prison and supported tenants living in poor housing, often in the inner-city suburbs of Ponsonby, Grey Lynn and Herne Bay. They produced a multilingual booklet called *Legal Aid*, written with the help of David Lange (a lawyer in Mangere, later to be prime minister) to help Pasifika people understand their rights when dealing with the police.

The Dawn Raids left a legacy of hurt, shame and heartache amongst the Pasifika population. Pasifika leaders and some church and other groups protested the raids at the time. The Polynesian Panther Party continued to call for an apology, including submitting a written request to the government, and in 2021, Prime Minister Jacinda Ardern issued a 'formal and unreserved apology' on behalf of the New Zealand government 'for the discriminatory implementation of the immigration laws of the 1970s that led to the events of the Dawn Raids'. Even 50 years later, she said, that legacy 'remains vividly etched in the memory of those who were directly impacted.'

Polynesian Panther Party *Legal Aid* booklet, c.1973–74.

Ref: 95-222-1/09-02, Alexander Turnbull Library, Wellington

> *Our Government conveys to the future generations of Aotearoa that the past actions of the Crown were wrong, and that the treatment of your ancestors was wrong. We convey to you our deepest and sincerest apology.*
>
> (Speech to Dawn Raids Apology, Rt Hon. Jacinda Ardern, 1 August 2021)

ESCAPING DANGER

REFUGEES AND ASYLUM SEEKERS

Refugees don't choose to leave their homes, but are forced to leave, often at short notice, because they are in danger.

New Zealand is one of the countries that has signed the 1951 Convention Relating to the Status of Refugees. The Refugee Convention and its 1967 Protocol explain who is a refugee, their rights and the help and protection they are entitled to receive.

A refugee is a person who:

- is outside his or her country of nationality or habitual residence
- has a well-founded fear of being persecuted because of his or her race, religion, nationality, membership of a particular social group or political opinion
- is unable or unwilling to avail himself or herself of the protection of that country, or to return there, for fear of persecution.

Refugees come to New Zealand under one of three categories: quota refugees, family members or asylum seekers. There are also special categories for refugees with high needs such as Medical/Disabled and Women at Risk.

New Zealand has resettled over 35,000 refugees since the Chinese wives and children (who came on temporary permits) and the Polish children arrived here during World War II. Today, refugees

Ethiopian refugees embrace at their reunion at Wellington Airport after being separated for 15 months.

Ref: EP/2000/0980/32-F, The Dominion Post Collection, Alexander Turnbull Library, Wellington

spend their first five weeks at Te Āhuru Mōwai o Aotearoa (Mangere Refugee Resettlement Centre) where they attend English language classes and learn about schools, bank accounts, how to get medical help and how to find work. From the Centre, they go to their new homes around the country.

The category of 'climate change refugee' does not yet legally exist, but in the future, there might be people whose homes become unliveable because of climate change. Pacific island nations such as Tuvalu are already seeing their land disappearing as sea levels rise.

Vietnam

By the end of the Vietnam War, the Viet Cong had taken over the capital, Saigon (now Ho Chi Minh City) and created the Socialist Republic of Vietnam. Many South Vietnamese were afraid to stay under communist rule and risked

The Buivan family from Vietnam in their Wellington dairy, 1982.

Ref: EP/1982/2248/4A-F, The *Dominion Post* Collection, Alexander Turnbull Library, Wellington

their lives stealing away in secret in small fishing boats. In 1977, 412 Vietnamese refugees arrived in New Zealand, and about 1500 more arrived in 1979 and 1980.

Old Russians

The Old Believers were Orthodox Christians who left Russia for China, then Hong Kong, when they were persecuted for their beliefs. In July 1965, about 100 Old Believers arrived in Christchurch and were settled in Invercargill, where there were already some other Russian families.

Uganda

In 1971, President Idi Amin took power in Uganda. Over the next eight years he ordered thousands of people to be killed, including journalists, artists, teachers and medical workers. He also expelled people who were

Refugees arriving from Uganda, Wellington Airport, 1972.

Ref: EP/1972/5327/5-F, Alexander Turnbull Library, Wellington; Stuff Limited

of Asian, not African origin. More than 200 Ugandan Asians came as refugees to New Zealand in 1972 and 1973.

Chile

On 11 September 1973 there was a military coup in Chile and the army, under General Augusto Pinochet, took over. People who supported former president Salvador Allende were arrested, imprisoned and tortured. Thousands were killed or simply disappeared. Others fled and some came to New Zealand as political refugees. Today, people from from Brazil, Argentina, Peru, Colombia, Uruguay, Bolivia and Venezuela live in New Zealand.

Colombian people at a multicultural festival in Tauranga.

Michael Williams, Dreamstime

Cambodia

The Khmer Rouge, under leader Pol Pot, seized power in 1975. Up to two million Cambodian people died of disease, starvation or overwork or were killed on Pol Pot's orders. Some people managed to cross the border to refugee camps in Thailand. About 4500 Cambodian refugees came to New Zealand from 1979 to 1992.

Somalia

Somalia was hit by drought, famine and civil war in the late 1980s and thousands fled to refugee camps in nearby countries. Somali people are Muslim and eat halal food and some women wear the hijab and head scarves. All these things were less common in New Zealand when the first Somali refugees arrived in 1993. Today there are about 1800 Somali people living mostly in Auckland, Hamilton and Wellington.

Bhutan

Bhutan is a small, beautiful and remote country in the Himalayas. In the 1980s, the Bhutanese government brought in a policy called 'One nation, one people'. In its first-ever census in 1988, many people were reclassified as illegal immigrants. These people, the Lhotshampa, were descended from Nepalis who came to Bhutan over a hundred years before. When their right to live in Bhutan was suddenly taken away, they fled or were forced to leave and to promise they would never return. New Zealand was the first country to accept refugees from Bhutan. The first 75 arrived in 2008 and since then, several hundred have settled here.

Cambodian refugees at Kelvin Grove Community Hall, Palmerston North, 1993.

COMM1482197375, Manawatū Heritage Community Archives, Sivlean Ung, 1993

Somali refugee family in Naenae, Lower Hutt.

Ref: EP/1998/1362/15-F, The Dominion Post Collection, Alexander Turnbull Library, Wellington

Rwanda

Rwanda is one of the smallest countries in Africa. In 1994, it was caught up in a bitter war between two tribes, the Hutus and Tutsis. As many as 800,000 people were killed out of a total population of six million. Many Tutsi were killed by Hutu, even if they had been neighbours and friends, but other Hutu people sheltered and hid Tutsi and saved their lives. People fled to refugee camps in neighbouring countries and some of those refugees later came to New Zealand.

Assyrian Christians

Once a powerful Empire, Assyria no longer exists as a country, but its people hold fast to their culture, language, faith and even their flag. Assyrian refugees first came to New Zealand in the 1980s and 1990s after fleeing the Iran-Iraq war and the Gulf wars. In 1989 there were only 10 Assyrian families in Wellington, but now there is a close community of about 2500 people with their own church, language school, radio show and men's and women's football teams. Altogether there are about 5000 Assyrians living in New Zealand.

South Asia

The *Tampa*, a Norwegian container ship, was sailing across the Indian Ocean when, on 26 August 2001, it came across a wooden fishing boat that was close to sinking. The *Palapa* had set off from Indonesia towards the Australian territory of Christmas Island but its engines had failed. Its 433 passengers, including children and pregnant women, came from Afghanistan, Pakistan and Sri Lanka.

Captain Arne Rinnan took them all on board. The Australian government said they would not let the asylum seekers ashore at Christmas Island; some of the passengers agreed to return home and some spent years on Nauru at a detention centre. Prime Minister Helen Clark offered to let some of the people into New Zealand and the first group arrived in September 2001. Altogether New Zealand accepted 131 of the *Tampa* boat people. They were mainly Afghani (from a minority ethnic group called Hazara) and mostly families and teenage boys, and were later given refugee status.

Helen Clark, then United Nations High Commissioner for Refugees, at the ceremony in 2005 when 76 *Tampa* refugees were granted New Zealand citizenship.

John Selkirk

1987 TO TODAY

IMMIGRATION ACT 1987

Until 1920, New Zealand's immigration policy was set out in legislation, but this changed with the permit system brought in by the Immigration Restriction Amendment Act 1920. Immigration policy was no longer publicly available in the form of Acts and Regulations. Instead, decisions were made behind the scenes by government ministers and officials. A memorandum on 'Immigration into New Zealand: International Problems' from the Prime Minister's Department stated:

> *Our immigration policy is based firmly on the principle that we are and intend to remain a country of European development. It is inevitably discriminatory against Asians — indeed against all persons who are not wholly of European race and colour. Whereas we have done much to encourage immigration from Europe, we do everything to discourage it from Asia.*
> (Dept of External Affairs, PM 32/3/1, Part 8; 1952–53, Archives NZ)

Apart from one Immigration Act in 1964, there was no legislative change for decades, but in the 1970s and 1980s there were new economic factors to consider. In 1971, the Leader of the Opposition (later Labour prime minister) Norman Kirk recognised that 'New Zealand's future lay with Asia and the Pacific' and called for 'the development of a two-way immigration policy based on equality and ignoring questions of race, colour and religion'. (*Press*, June 1971)

The Immigration Policy Review of 1986 led to the Immigration Act 1987, passed by the Labour government under Prime Minister David Lange. There was no longer a preference, stated or implied, for migrants from Britain, Europe or other Western countries. Instead, immigration was to be based on merit and job skills. An occupational priority list highlighted the skills that were needed.

In 1991 the National government passed the Immigration Amendment Act, which removed the priority list and established a points system based on factors such as qualifications, work experience and age. In 1995, an English language test was added with a minimum score needed. The pass mark for the points system could be adjusted year by year so there was no mark that guaranteed entry.

From the late 1980s, immigrants began to arrive from Asia: China, Taiwan, Hong Kong, India, Malaysia, Singapore, South Korea and the Philippines. In the 20 years between the 1986 and 2006 censuses, the number of New Zealand Asian-born residents increased from about 30,000 to about 250,000. One consequence of this was that the predominant Chinese language used here gradually changed from Cantonese to Mandarin.

This transformed New Zealand's cultural demography and reactions were not always positive. New Asian migrants were blamed for everything from expensive housing and changing school populations to bad driving. When Covid-19 began to spread in 2020, some Asian New Zealanders felt discriminated against or blamed for the impact of the virus.

MIGRANT WORKERS

For many years, Pasifika and Asian people came to New Zealand as seasonal workers under Pacific Work Schemes or on ordinary work visas and permits. The Recognised Seasonal Employer (RSE) initiative began in 2007, aimed at people from Vanuatu, Samoa, Tonga, Fiji, Tuvalu and Kiribati. These workers left their homes to work in orchards and vineyards in the Bay of Plenty, Hawke's Bay, Nelson, Marlborough and Central Otago.

Ni-Vanuatu workers, Blenheim.
Johnny Blades/RNZ Pacific

Dairy workers from the Philippines began arriving in New Zealand in the early 2000s. Many settled in Canterbury and Southland where they set up organisations to support their members, uphold Filipino traditions and help settle new arrivals. Invercargill is home to a large number of Filipino migrants working in nursing, caregiving, welding and farming, and there are Filipino speciality grocery stores and cafés.

COLOMBO PLAN AND OTHER STUDENTS

The Colombo Plan began in 1950 at a Commonwealth meeting in Colombo, Ceylon (now Sri Lanka) to discuss ways to support the countries of South and South-East Asia. One idea was to send students to study overseas, so they could go back to their own country and help in its development. The first Colombo Plan students, six dental nurse trainees from

Ceylon, arrived in New Zealand in March 1951. The students lived in hostels or boarded with families. For many, it was their first time overseas. They got a monthly allowance for living costs, extra grants for books and clothing, and could even apply for a 'blanket grant', because it was often colder than at home.

Many other international students came here to study at schools, universities, polytechnics and training institutions, but Covid-19 had a huge impact. In March 2020, at the start of the pandemic, there were about 60,000 international students here. In July 2022, when the borders fully reopened, their numbers had dropped to 14,639.

Colombo Plan students in Wellington, 1960.

Ref: EP/1960/0161-F, The Dominion Post Collection, Alexander Turnbull Library, Wellington

THE IMPACT OF COVID-19 ON MIGRATION

For decades, people have arrived, left and returned, but when the Covid-19 pandemic began to spread across the world, New Zealanders overseas scrambled to get home before borders were shut or airlines grounded. Over two months, 80,000 New Zealanders returned home but some families were separated for months or years.

From 11.59 p.m. on 19 March 2020, and for the first time in New Zealand's history, its borders were closed to anyone except New Zealand citizens or permanent residents and their children or partners. On Monday 18 May 2020, nobody arrived or left the country for the first time since the 1960s.

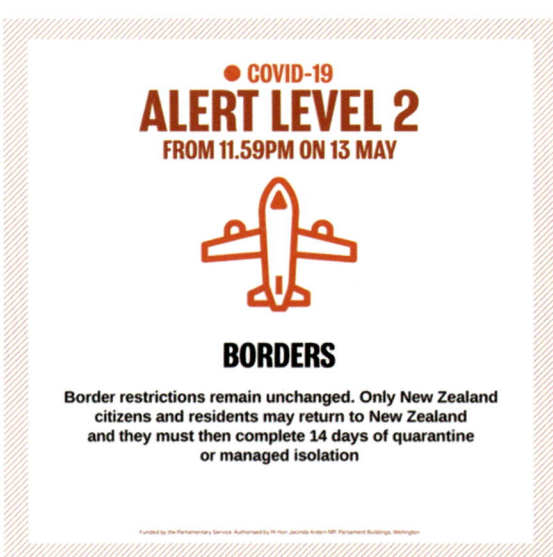

At the same time, many travellers stayed longer than they had intended because of Covid-related travel and border restrictions, both here and overseas. In the year ended March 2020, this resulted in a record net gain of 91,700 people, the highest it has ever been.

Usually more than 5500 people, or 15% of the workforce on dairy farms were skilled migrant workers. Some had gone home to see their families. With the borders shut, they couldn't get back and their employers had no one to work the farms at the busiest time of year. Others were trapped because there were no flights home, or the flights were very expensive. Refugees were stuck in refugee camps, even if they had been accepted to come here.

CELEBRATING DIVERSITY

New migrants treasure the traditions from their homeland. Food, festivals, music, dance and keeping the language alive are ways to maintain their cultural heritage.

Today you can find Italian pizza and pasta, Greek yoghurt, French baguettes, South African biltong, Chinese vegetables, dumplings and wontons, Malaysian noodles, Vietnamese spring rolls and pho, Japanese sushi and ramen, Thai green curries, Indian samosa and dosa, Turkish kebabs, Mexican tacos, Dutch liquorice and windmill cookies, Ethiopian injera, Taiwanese bubble tea and many other dishes that weren't available when migrants from those countries first arrived.

Running race at Ambedkar Sports Day, Pukekohe, 2008.
ASC-D-2008-039, Auckland Libraries Heritage Collections

TOP AND ABOVE Pasifika Festival, 2023.

C. Lagahetau

Some festivals are huge, such as the Chinese New Year Lantern Festival and the Pasifika Festival in Auckland. Some are celebrated nationwide, like Eid or Diwali. Other festivals are small and local, like the Blessing of the Boats, an Italian tradition first held in Island Bay, Wellington, in 1933 after the fishing boat *Santina* and its crew were lost in Cook Strait.

People celebrate their home country's Independence Day or Language Week. Vietnamese mark Lunar New Year (Tet Nguyen Dan) and the Mid-Autumn Festival, also called the Children's Festival (Tet Trung Thu). Iranian people celebrate Nowruz, which means 'new day' in Farsi and marks the arrival of spring and the New Year. Orthodox Christians (such as Greek and Ethiopian) have a different date for Easter. Other celebrations include White Sunday (Pasifika), Tulip Sunday and Sinterklaas (Dutch), St Patrick's Day (Irish),

Highland Games (Scottish) and the Up Helly Aa fire festival (Shetland Islands).

Museums often have collections relating to people from the area. Some museums focus on specific groups: gum diggers (Kauri Museum, Matakohe), Scottish Highlanders (Waipu Museum), Polish children (Polish Heritage Trust Museum, Auckland) and Dutch migrants (Oranjehof Dutch museum and De Molen windmill in Foxton).

Central Otago has several remains of Chinese mining camps and settlements, such as the Lawrence Chinese camp, established in 1866 on the edge of town because Chinese miners were not allowed to live in Lawrence itself. A small stone hut built into the cliffs at the Illustrious Energy Hut Historic Area, near Alexandra, is typical of the ones lived in by Chinese miners. Gay Tan's house at Macraes Flat belonged to Louis Gay Tan (Looi Yi Tsaan) who arrived in

BELOW De Molen Dutch Windmill, Foxton.
Richair, Dreamstime

BOTTOM Chinese Lantern Festival, Auckland.
Patrimonio Designs Limited, Dreamstime

Otago in 1867. He married a European, Emma Finch, and was a manager of mine workers on the gold fields. The Ng King Brothers Chinese Market Garden Settlement in Ashburton is a unique example of a market garden that was the hub of the local Chinese community from the 1920s until it closed in 1964.

BELOW Group of young performers celebrating Diwali.
Michael Williams, Dreamstime

BOTTOM Highland dancers at a Highland Games event.
Gina Smith, Dreamstime

Cemeteries are full of stories. Some old cemeteries had separate sections for Chinese. The Chinese headstones in the Lawrence cemetery were overgrown and forgotten about for years but have now been restored.

Memorials can tell stories. Matiu Island in Te Whanganui-a-Tara/Wellington Harbour was once a quarantine station. Memorials there record the names of those who survived the long journey on sailing ships but died of illness before they could go ashore.

Place names tell stories. Some names refer back to the journey of Kupe; other places are named after early European explorers. Dunedin was named after the Gaelic form of Edinburgh, Scotland's capital. Streets can hold clues to local history. In Akaroa, where French settlers arrived on 15 August 1840, there are French street signs such as Rue Jolie, Rue Benoit and Rue Lavaud. Nelson has Italian street names and Cashmere in Christchurch has Indian street names. The country's first bilingual street sign, in English and Cantonese script, is Jean Hing Place, Ōtaki, located on the site of a Chinese market garden.

Nowruz, the celebration of New Year in Iran, is a time for music, food and dancing.

Forough Amin, Iranian Women in NZ

CONCLUSION

New Zealand is a small island nation. Everyone who lives here either came from somewhere else or is descended from people who at some stage came from somewhere else.

According to the 2018 census, 27.4% of the population of Aotearoa New Zealand, or more than a quarter, were born overseas. The Auckland region had 33.4% (one third) of the total population and 50.7% of those, or just over half, were born overseas. This makes Auckland one of the most super diverse cities in the world. (A 'super diverse' city is defined as one where 25% or more of the population were born overseas.)

New Zealand's Parliament is becoming more representative of its migrant population. Golriz Ghahraman became the first refugee MP in 2017. Her family arrived here from Iran as asylum seekers in 1990. Members of Parliament after the 2020 election included New Zealand's first African (from Eritrea), Latin American (from Mexico) and Sri Lankan MPs as well as Māori, Pasifika and MPs from China, India, Korea and the Maldives.

For millions of years, there were no people living in New Zealand. Now there are over five million of us. All of us can say: 'We came from far away, but New Zealand is our home now.'

Thousands of people attend the annual International Cultural Festival in Auckland.

Jason Dorday, *The New Zealand Herald*

He aha te mea nui o te ao?
He tangata! He tangata! He tangata!
What is the most important thing in the world?
It is people! It is people! It is people!

Māori whakataukī

INDEX

Aliens 34, 40–41, 52, 53
Ashburton 96
Assisted passage 19, 21, 22, 24–25, 27, 64–66
Auckland 23, 51, 77, 98
Austrian migrants 65–66

Bay of Islands 17, 20
Bay of Plenty 89
British migrants 19–26, 34, 57–58, 64–65

Campbell Island 33
Canterbury 19, 31, 51, 90
Cartography 14
Chain migration 68
Child migrants 55–59, 64–65
Chinese migrants 34–40, 43–47, 58–59, 89, 95–96, 97
Christchurch 48, 97
Colombo Plan 90–91
Colonisation 19–21, 23–24, 25, 71
Competition 13
Cook, Captain James 14, 15
Covid-19 89, 91, 92

Dalmatian migrants 29–31, 40
Dannevirke 29
Dawn Raids 78–79
Disability 41–42, 80
Diversity 93–97
Dogs 11, 32–33
Dusky Sound 15
Dutch migrants 70–71

Earliest arrivals 8–13
European arrivals 14–17, 19–22, 23, 26, 27–33, 34, 40–41, 54–58, 60–61, 64–71

Fiji Indian migrants 51
Filipino migrants 90
Food 10, 11–12, 15, 16, 17, 18, 28, 45, 47, 49, 54, 68, 93
Forestry 12, 17, 27, 29–31
French migrants 14–15, 97

German migrants 41, 51–53
Gold mining 44, 49, 66, 96
Greek migrants 68–69
Gum digging 29, 30–31, 40, 95

Hawaiki 13
Hawke's Bay 28, 89

'Hindus' 40
Hostels 57, 75–76

Indian migrants 16, 34, 39, 42, 48–51, 94, 96, 97
Intermarriage 13, 16, 31, 39, 59–60, 96
Internal migration 13, 25
Introduced species 11, 32
Invercargill 82, 90
Italian migrants 66–68, 97

Jewish migrants 54

Kōpuaranga 28
Kororāreka (Russell) 17
Kupe 8, 9

Land disputes 13, 20, 21, 23, 42, 71–72
Land surveyors 24
Language 14, 17–18, 37, 39–40, 41, 42, 44, 45, 49, 64, 89, 97
Legislation 25, 31, 36–37, 38–42, 44–45, 49, 54, 73, 80, 88–89
Lyttelton 22

Mackenzie, James 32–33
Māori 8–13, 14, 16–18, 20–21, 24, 25, 31, 40, 51, 71–76, 78
Matiu/Somes Island 28, 31, 52, 53, 97
Mellemskov (Eketahuna) 29
Military settlers 23
Missionaries 17–18, 66
Moriori 11
Motuihe Island 53

New Plymouth 19
New Zealand Company 19–22
New Zealand Indian Central Association 42
New Zealand Wars 23, 25
Norsewood 29
Nova Scotia 33

Otago 19, 32, 44, 46, 49, 89, 95

Pākehā Māori 16
Parkhurst boys 23
Pasifika 77–79, 81, 89, 94
'Pepper potting' 73–74

Polish migrants 55–57, 95
Polynesian Panther Party 78–79
Population 13, 17, 26, 45, 49, 71, 72, 77, 84, 85, 87, 89, 92, 98
Provincial government 20, 24–25
Pukekohe 42, 73

Racism 34–41, 42, 45, 46–47, 49, 72–73, 78–79, 88, 89
Railways 25, 26, 29
Rakiura/Stewart Island 16, 33
Refugees 42, 54–57, 58–59, 60–61, 80–87, 92, 98
Rēkohu/Chatham Islands 11
Remutaka Hill 28

Scandinavian migrants 27–29
Scottish migrants 31–33, 96, 97
Sealers 15–16
Seventy Mile Bush 27, 29
Slavery 13, 17
Southland 51, 90

Te Ara-a-Kiwa/Foveaux Strait 16
Te Tiriti o Waitangi/Treaty of Waitangi 17, 20, 21
Traders 13, 17, 20, 28, 33, 50, 71

Urban migration 71–76

Vogel, Julius 25

Waipu 33
Waitangi Tribunal 21
Wellington 19, 20, 35, 57, 66, 67
Whakatāne 10
Whakatū/Nelson 19, 43, 49, 89
Whalers 15–16, 17
Whenua Hou/Codfish Island 16–17
White New Zealand League 35, 42
Women 8, 10, 16, 17, 20, 21, 23, 24, 28, 39–40, 45, 46, 49–50, 59–60, 67, 69, 75, 80

'Yellow peril' 34–35